FAMILY IN PERU

FAMILY IN PERU

by

JOHN SYKES

THE TRAVEL BOOK CLUB
121 CHARING CROSS ROAD
LONDON W.C.2

First published in 1962
Anthony Blond Ltd

MADE AND PRINTED IN GREAT BRITAIN BY
THE GARDEN CITY PRESS LIMITED
LETCHWORTH, HERTFORDSHIRE

for Danny

CONTENTS

1

PRELIMINARIES

Two centuries ago a traveller to Lima remarked that it was enough to be the friend of their godfather's cousin's adopted son, last heard of fighting in Europe, to be received royally by a family. The least whiff of an introduction and their house and goods were at your feet. It might only last the space of an evening, fading out in equal style, or it might see you through your stay in their country. That depended on how things went.

With this thought in mind, for in my pocket I carried the vaguest of introductions, I left the hotel and the first perimeter of airline offices and souvenir shops and turned up one of the narrower streets in search of a quiet coffee. At first sight I didn't like Lima. But that might be fatigue from flying and disappointment at coming down from the brilliant spring day above the clouds to the damp colourless climate of the city. Up there the eagle glory of the Andes, down here what could be Manchester. Also the company of a shoal of tourists with their schedule round the continent fixed, a morning here, an afternoon there with private car and chauffeur-guide, not only inclined one to expect wonders and to write off what didn't amaze, but already to be so involved with tomorrow as to feel impatient about today.

I bought an armful of Peruvian papers and settled into a coffee house where the utterly natural politeness of the waiter was a first nudge back to normality.

It is wonderful, after travelling under pressure, suddenly to go slack. No more last-minute dash to the airport, only to fidget for another hour; no more queueing for immigration, no more pacing the lounge at midnight staring into illuminated showcases. An end to porters, even orange juice. How quickly one forgot, as in time of war, the usual conveniences of being alive. How nice to feel life twitching back.

But it takes a while for all that to slough off, to be relaxed and awake again. I was sipping the coffee and reading the first paper and bemusedly staring at the passing street, the front of my mind still a hum and a blur of touching down and soaring upwards; and I couldn't forget the splendour of the mountains, the condor's view of Latin America, with Pacific foam against a strip of desert rising to chain upon chain of peaks, bleak rasping promontories and high interlocking valleys, from above a vertiginously narrow sequence, for immediately to the east lay the Amazon jungle like a vast steamy sunken garden, stretching endlessly towards the Atlantic.

For hours above that cordillera, with snow-filled sunshine and wads of cloud forming in advance of the rainy season, I had brooded ahead to the coming months of journeying up and down the Andes, at least that part within range of Lima, and of seeing something of local customs before they disappeared from the world. One had to be pretty nippy these days, with the world dissolving into one. And though I knew my schoolday picture of Peru, golden with Incas and Conquistadors, would meet with wholesale modification, I really knew very little else. I had purposely kept away from books, and in Europe Latin American countries were seldom intelligently talked about. Between most of us and them stood the image of Spain, or the State Department, and now Castro. I wanted my own visual impressions and to pick up threads of local feeling. Hence the value of my introduction, so as to cross to the inside.

I was only half-looking at the papers and only half-looking at the street—so persistent still the sensation of the flight—but I was becoming conscious in the passers-by of a rather marked strain and anxiety, as though they had all been saddled with sums their heads could not quite cope with, and of traffic wearyingly edging past and finally jammed so that an ancient bus, salvaged, one would say, from a river bed, was panting black fumes through the doorway, till my coffee and saucer, a neighbour's cream cake, the table, my fingers, the recesses of my shirt began to freckle with fine deposit. The air was murderously unwholesome. But, as in Leeds and Sheffield with the smog that settles about three in the afternoon, nobody appeared to notice. Outside the harassed faces passed, for the most part hieratically silent, locked in their hopeless mathematics; while within the soft high voices, complaining, extolling, exaggerating, continued at a canter.

The bus shuddered forward. The following queue strained for the lights, to be stopped again; bringing an equally ancient bus, shaking with fumes and bulging above the pavement, to put the café back in shadow.

The newspapers added to the tension, but clamorously, at the top of their voice: their news like so many public speakers or auctioneers haranguing the reader, boxing his ears (the two leading dailies were principally boxing one another) with accusations of political fraud and insults against the national honour, with frontier incidents, police incidents, rot in the Treasury and the universities, with the sewer-like misery of the city slums to be remedied (but here the language grew tangled) by the XYZ million dollar programme: and all laced with high life parties, football dramas, and a catch of films advertised as unsuitable for women.

Was anyone expected to swallow, even to read, half these outpourings? Or were they there rather because someone needed to pour them out, to grab the stage and sob and scream: a sort of public analyst's couch? No one in view carried a paper. All, silent or prattling away, were utterly engrossed in themselves.

However, in the radical Press, from liberal pink to blatant red, there were at least articles and news dealing with events outside the main cities. There was a sudden breath of country air, and the figure of the peasant appeared. For the big dailies he didn't exist except as a vague statistical worry; though even I knew that, in the main Indian, he was the salt and savour of the Peruvian people, sixty per cent of their population. Here too of course he was being used—for these papers were written by angry intellectuals—as a stick to beat the all-powerful rich, but at east he was here. His existence was acknowledged. And if a hundredth part of this news was true, in the remote valleys and plateaux of his history, he was still an extraordinarily heroic figure.

What for instance could one make of this, among the general rumbling of revolt and arrests, an item rather soberly reported by a local peasant Federation as having led to trouble near Cuzco? It said that a leading landowner there not only had forced his peons to work sixteen hours at a stretch per day, had imprisoned one, whipped another senseless, but had compelled five of them to run before his mule so that he could trample them down repeatedly; and another time had saddled a man, loaded him with coffee bags and lashed him round the hacienda yard; and another time had strung a man up by hands and feet and whipped him till his own sons had begged him to stop.

Could this be true, this petty fascism, this suggestion of an African convict farm? Modern horror is such that we are all a bit numbed and sceptical in consequence, but frankly this item woke me up. Gone now all airborne vagueness. Turning again through the papers I could see that this report, though extreme, was not out of key with the tenor of affairs. Police bullets, landowners' whips, political chicanery, urban frustration: it added up to an initial picture. I had been dreaming simply of a congenial visit, but this was the first strong stink of reality.

I paid and joined the anxious street. I now not only disliked Lima but felt an aversion to the whole of Peru. What a revolting feudal mess. Of course it could only be part of the scene, perhaps rapidly being transformed. There were clearly people who did not condone it, the majority probably, certainly those with whom I hoped to enjoy myself. I had obviously got it out of proportion. For I had only been two hours in the country and by chance and not in the brightest of moods dipping into some left-wing papers.

I really mustn't start to fall foul of a travel prospect nursed over years. What a long way to come for that.

The street was still jammed with traffic, choked with rancid fumes; though even those in chauffeur-driven cars, even those in the lengthening queues, seemed to be simply unaware of it. Or was perhaps that they knew the futility of giving it a thought.

I dived into the nearest church.

Peace, at least. No answers to problems, to the doubts so harshly raised so soon, but peace, and high vaulting shadows and the red-reflecting flicker of candles. The black mantillas of kneeling women. What muttering there was softened and transmuted into an effect of centred prayer. One's own preoccupations stilled.

I sat down and felt quieter. No answers. Simply this.

Emerging I found, by parallel chance, that the town had changed too. It was dusk, softer, and the main street had been turned over to pedestrians. People were laughing, there was a play of gesture as if messages were being passed down a line. How fast everyone was talking! But moving slowly, the girls using all the space around them for expression. Where had these pretty girls been before? They looked so amused to be alive, so ready for a lark, and they were vanishing into bars and cinemas, stepping to the street-long hum of mambos, and in the main moving to the square ahead. Above in the sky the darkening grey was cut by bands of faint yellow.

I decided to phone the friend of a friend, to chance my introduction.

"But my dear Señor," came his voice, in the soft Latin American Spanish, "we have been expecting you for over a week. Why are you so terribly delayed! But what luck, for tonight we have a party."

Later, when I knew more about Infantes, though I didn't need to know much to know this, I was to learn that every night he had a party: but like all Peruvians, and especially at that moment, he made it sound like a present for me.

Easier than his driving in to fetch me, and easier at that hour than my looking for a taxi, was for me to make the quarter of an hour journey to Miraflores by collectivo. That was simply a fixed-run taxi in which for the fixed sum of about sixpence one took one of the five places and got off at any point one chose.

He explained it: if down Avenida Arequipa, the channel of this particular run, one wanted house 4036, or some such number in a parallel street, one told the driver to put one down at the corner of the fortieth block and walked on thirty-six metres: a fastidiously Roman idea. In this case, however, I was to do the whole run.

To get the collectivo I had to join a queue, and there was time to think what a great contribution collectivos could make to London, radiating from central points to Hampstead, Chelsea, Hammersmith, Croydon, reducing the single-passenger traffic. They are in fact to be met with up and down the world, a cab service at bus prices—though what a war that would start in England! At least another century must pass.

Plaza San Martin by night, for night had fallen, and without the chill of the late afternoon, was ringed by advertising lights on a front of buildings four storeys high, with café arcades on two sides, and the main hotel, the main foreign company, the main club, the main cinemas, placed around like watchful beadles. In the centre was a vast walking space, but not so much astroll with couples as somersaulting with shoeshine boys, and even younger children with a bowl of soup while their mothers sold papers and sweets, and with waifs who begged wandering mechanically from one unknown adult to another. A hum of traffic, though moderated, filled the scene and additionally gave it the soft rill of the policeman's whistle, throaty, intermittent, like a bird in a tree—no townsman's whistle, that.

There was, I suppose, sufficient in the scene to make a stranger perturbed again, and I have omitted the tommy gun police, in different uniforms and with a different kind of face, who had appeared as if at the call of night at all four corners of the square; but mood, conscience, feeling involved, is wayward and at that moment for me was caught in delight at being alive, on a spring evening in a strange country, which somehow doubly confirmed one's existence, and with a welcome to the hours ahead.

"Maestro, cobre se." Each of us in turn uttered the formula, usually just before getting out, as we handed two soles (about sixpence) to the driver. "Maestro, collect your due." With military precision the cabs ran up, took on passengers, and were signalled away; and with a flair that could not bear to waste an inch of ground or an ounce of speed they joined like a pack at the exit of the square, bluffed and shot over intersections, swerved in mad racing concourse round a zone of parks and museums, then tally-ho down the straight to Miraflores.

Buildings, trees, electric signs, came at us like missiles. A passenger indicated his corner, the cab slowed, and as it stopped, if necessary others would alight first to make his exit easier; equally, if at the next corner someone answered the driver's signal, made by the free arm motioning forward to show there was a spare place inside, then again in terms of stops to come, if it would make things easier then, someone alighted so as to let the newcomer straight into the middle. All done with ease and manners that, though unsmiling, for, close to, these first companions looked dead beat, glistened with accustomed polish. "Buenos tardes!" Each gave his greeting, and was greeted in return by the driver. There was next to no conversation. For besides fatigue, as earlier in the street, each appeared locked in himself, or perhaps in some enormous grudge or uncertainty. But none of this tarnished the surface: the respect and charm due to others. Speak a word, ask a question, and the reply caressed you as if from a lifetime's reverent acquaintance. Each of us was Señor or Señora, the holy vessel of a personality.

"Mi amor . . ." hummed the radio, in loose-limbed syncopation.

The cool evening blew through the window.

Miraflores was another fairway of lights. The last three of us left the cab. So strong the atmosphere of the journey, so personal, however enclosed each person, whatever he carried of the background horror embedded deep within his being, that I hesitated . . . surely now the three of us must have a drink together? To mark what to an Englishman seemed an unusual display of sympathy at sight?

But they had gone. All in the day's performance. Another five impeccable Limeñans, thrusting yet seeming to assist each other, were filling the cab for the return run. The driver thumped the outside of his door to urge on a lagging car ahead. The warm cocoon was off. A dozen others sped after it.

The party for the evening looked as though it had started in the afternoon, or perhaps the day, perhaps the year before. There was a scatter of used ashtrays and glasses and cushions that at some point had been sat on. It was a large smokily lit room with the most advanced lighting conceptions, recessed corners, screens, a well that led to french windows and a garden, and varying tones of colour on the walls. It was the main living space of a flat that might have turned up in Paris, appropriately enough for the owner was a painter, his studio or call it his working area half-screened off in a corner; and he appropriately jeaned in black, with a polo sweater, and the look of an athlete who got his ideas while vaulting through the air.

His wife when I entered was also in jeans, but shortly reappeared in a dress, bewitchingly petite, as if to signal some progression otherwise unapparent; for a guest had left but not without saying that he might be back later with friends, and a couple had followed in after me but as if they had just been out for a breather, while the other four guests looked to have been talking, purring at each other and playing records, since this wonderful room had come into being. The painter from time to time might paint, measuring his canvas into verticals of colour or into concentric tonal boxes, such as the two examples on view; and his wife might every so often change, or phone, or give instructions to the maid about little bits of food to bring in; but otherwise the set wouldn't alter, there would always be talk and music in the background, creating the bohemia that for them was as much of Paris or Rome or New York as Lima. As a European I was effusively greeted.

I had discovered that my host was not Infantes, but his friend and teacher, Enrique Roda. Infantes had risen from a corner to explain: Roda Ugarte was the master of them all and had just broken through to a new style. More than ever therefore they congregated here, so he had simply given me this address—as someone might say, meet me at the Dôme.

"Su casa, Señor," chimed in Roda. "It is your house. Please to feel at home."

I already did, it was so like Hampstead, accepting from the plates Señora Roda was offering. A sort of kebab called anticuchos, white cheese, olives, wine: and with this a barter of London news for local information.

She was small-boned, dainty-fingered, light of speech, epicurean. Her face was pale, and so black her hair and so animated her tiny eyes that against them her cheeks seemed to fade out. Her desire, I believe, was to seem blasé, but this was spoilt by evident need to proclaim the good standing and sensibility of herself and everyone else present, and to scent out my affairs. It was necessary to be very tactful.

Infantes, who had a ridiculous moustache, could not help much, and I would even say that he had shot his bolt of kindness for the evening; as after all he knew nothing about me except that I was a friend of a friend. But here the Señora, once I had satisfied a few innocently phrased questions, herself underpinned the position, introducing me to the next arrival as "a very good friend of Infantes", and later as "our friend from London". By now she knew that I was married, had children, suffered from a hopeless passion for travel, and was curious about Andean Indian culture. To her this meant I was an archeologist. "Oh, los pobres," she murmured, "what remains to them? You will see for yourself at Machu Picchu!"

"Though," she returned to her own reality, "what remains for anyone here? Lima is losing its especial quality. It is no longer the city of Ricardo Palma. We must see to it that you are not too bored. How I wish we could move to New York for a time. We may, soon . . ."

Another guest entered. By now I had become "my English friend".

Flattering though this was I also suspected it might not outlast the evening.

I should be back sitting in fume-choked cafés.

This prospect, however, was averted by Roda. He had been circling the room like a leashed panther, unable perhaps to tackle a canvas but irritated by everything else: though like everyone here his smile was uppermost, supple, feline, careful of the tone conserved by this bohemia. He descended on us, caught his wife sighing as she struggled to see any future for Peru, and murmured, "The future is in the past!"—circled, while this shaft like a vodka worked on the appreciative mind of Infantes, then joined us with a sudden explosion of ideas, of rapier questioning and judo tumbling of half the points he himself raised: a virtuoso performance that left him sad, as this energy ought to have gone into a painting. But he was a kind man, in the backwash he asked me what it was I was really after; then exclaimed, "Ah si, you must meet Paula! She's the only one of us still who paints and thinks about the Indians. Sabogal—no, Mariategui .. he was the great inspiration for her. Though one never knows exactly with Paula . . ."

"Ah si, Paula . . ." his wife echoed, with an opposite intonation.

"Matilde Mármol's friend," said Infantes, elucidating, though not for me. "Though how can one tell with a Montellano? Look at Carlos! They're unpredictable."

"She's my cousin," said Roda, pinning it down. "I'll phone to see if she's at home now."

"She says," he smiled, returning in a minute, "that she has just got rid of some people. That she is going out to a cinema. That her husband is still in America. That she is in a bad mood. But that, anyway, we can all come round." He looked pleased with himself.

"You go," decided his wife, "and take Reynaldo." Reynaldo was Infantes. To me she extended a curious smile that was half grudging congratulation. "Anytime . . . you just ring us up. We might go to a museum. Or—come back later." She had dropped me momentarily.

I kissed her hand, as was the custom.

It was wonderful to be out in the air again, and the Cadillac at the kerbside, pleasantly enough, belonged to Infantes. Two others of the group were with us. They had been leaving, but seized this chance to go along; the air and the fuzz of lights and traffic and omnipresent click of mambo suggested endless continuations. We drove into an area of avenues and of villas that though each one different in style, with turrets or receding decks, with an arabesque of grilles or built about the garage, immense and standing twenty feet back or small and flush with the pavement, were all joined right around the block like the parapets of a medieval city, with a pool of gardens securely in the middle. One of these belonged to Paula, Paula Inés Montellano Roda de Alvano Graham, as her cousin flourished it. Their conversation danced the more brightly, soft and running and wicked with stories, as her name came into it. Señora Alvano! For what in the world had been the name of her first husband? Had he died or had she had it annulled? The Montellanos were always changing: partners, houses, enterprises. Basically, she was simply Paula.

What a pity she couldn't really paint!

Her house, next to a frontage of venetian blinds and gardened balconies, was a high sandy-coloured wall, surmounted by tiles and almond blossom, and a third of it rising to a second storey slit by two discreet windows. A brown-faced maid answered the bell.

"Enrique! What a delight to see you." Her moody face discounted the words. We had skirted a tree-filled courtyard, entered a hall and a couple of rooms that led one into the other, and were being attentively served with whisky. Otherwise she was ignoring us for him, though that too looked largely formal. She was a tall, wilful, melancholic woman, about thirty, slightly running to fat. As she spoke to you, seeming to discount you, you noticed an irreverent glint in her eyes, occupied with inner worlds. There was a portrait of a general hanging in the hall with just that same look to him.

There was a younger woman in the room, with an equally

grave face but vain, twisting in her seat and recrossing her legs
to show off her ravishing dress and figure. She smiled as though
she would gladly poison us, "Bobo's cross," scoffed Paula, as she
passed at one point in front of her. "We are not going to the
cinema."

She suggested we should follow her upstairs, where there
was something she wanted to show Roda. We filed, replenished
whiskies in hand, through the two rooms rather stiffly decorated:
high-backed chairs, cedar chests and tables, a resplendent crest-
topped mantelpiece, a showcase of fans, water colours, all so to
speak guarded by the general; then up the stairs lined with framed
colonial documents relating to her husband's father's family;
then into a small studio and snug, heaped with paintings and
bookshelves and examples of peasant pottery. On one wall hung
a brown and white vicuna rug, beneath it a settee, and suspended
to one side a filigree moorish lamp. The pottery, I was to learn,
came from the sierra, from Quinua and Pucará—clay-coloured
church façades and bulls, and black bulls of a startling vitality.
There was enough in these pieces to hold the eye, but so much else
in this treasure room—a painted carving of Christ on the Cross
of the earliest colonial period, swords crossed on the wall above
the door, embroidered cloths used for cushions, and a gaunt
modern sculpture by the window. It was a room for the satisfactions of memory, for coffee, as much as for creative work. But
it was to show one of her paintings that she had brought us.

Astride the easel—well, there were large square blobs of brown
receding like cottages down a street, and squiggles of black that
could be people, and an overall greyness binding sky and earth
in layers of thickness like torn-up paper. It had succeeded, perhaps; it was conscientious; the impasto was good and the tonality;
but it was hardly meat for this particular group of geometric
fundamentalists. As one of them showed by opening the stack of
earlier paintings, they preferred her definite men and women,
definite houses and hills and animals: even there formalised under
cubist inspiration by way of the Mexicans but endearingly dated,

in no way touching their own preoccuptions. But with these new blobs and squiggles . . . they were uneasy.

"Do you see, Enrique?" Her voice was sulky. It was a dry low-pitched voice. "Do you see the effect you have had on me?" She seemed to quiver; then as he began to murmur, speak, bristle with ideas of his own, in the way Enrique seemingly did, she turned from him, disappointed; and in a minute she had replaced her painting by an American's that she had recently purchased. That shook them with excitement.

It was then she started talking to me.

She was bored, annoyed, the curl to her mouth suggested she would seize on the first fatuity, let's say some expected traveller's question, to walk away from me too. "Which hotel . . . ? Do you like Lima? This climate . . . ?" Without listening to herself she was laying traps, speaking in English to make it easier for me to grate on her nerves enough. She wanted further irritation, like some drug addict shot by shot, to head towards still deeper gloom. I was so fascinated, however, by the setting, by her, actually by her expensive clothes, that I was hard put to it to reply at all. I was thinking, "Now that's just the very colour I wanted for my summer suit." Which has not, perhaps, much to do with travel.

She caught me staring intently at her in her own slightly remote way. As a traveller, I was not trying. She smiled. I smiled, and realised I had passed a test. From that point we hit it off.

Downstairs again, to get more whisky, she told Enrique that as he had ruined her evening he had better find another one for her. They began discussing possible parties. Seemingly, most evenings, there was a choice. "I think," she said, "there's one at home. For Consuelo. Mother mentioned it." It was immediately apparent that this had been part of her intention all along, perhaps after the cinema with Bobo (who had vanished), perhaps at the moment Enrique had phoned. This was not to be admitted, however; and for the next five minutes the two of them played the game of thinking up alternatives, discussing what it would be like at

Concha's, or Juan's, or the new nightclub, or down at Callao at that extraordinary restaurant . . . we could go for a walk, a walk round the docks!

With each less likely suggestion her humour improved; she became vivacious. She had a roguish, a fire-darting smile. She asked me: "But aren't we wasting your time, Señor? If you are here to study the Indians? Though, actually, we all have a touch —isn't that so, Enrique? The Spaniards landed here on a Monday, and by Tuesday we were a mestizo nation, You know, I think Mr Sykes ought to meet Puruvians who don't recognise that, who pretend to be barely aware of the 'natives', 'los animales' as they call them. That is the point to begin his study. We must open a few doors for him."

So that was how, with sudden manic decision, she brought me into her family circle: as a jest, though sharp-cutting somewhere, as her personal interpretation of how to help my Indian studies. This idea of "studies", by the way, originated with Roda, but I didn't disclaim it. Things were moving. We were already back in Infantes's car, heading for the Montellano mansion. I could see that if I had asked her directly about Cuzco (the scene of her paintings) or about Andean life, she would have been too bored even to reply: but this way she was enthusiastic. She was abrim with mischief. Play it like this and she was a guardian angel.

For me, as it turned out, though not without sadness, it was the key to my entire experience of Peru.

At the gate, a fine baroque construction set in a massive white wall, Roda and the others declined to come in—so that I half-guessed they had not been meant to, not as a group, anyway, here. She was saying how she would ring him tomorrow. Then she took me through as her friend.

The servant at the gate, a gigantic negro, dressed in the livery of the house, in other days could have been an executioner. Come to think of it, the small courtyard we had entered, aglow with lamps and with light from a balcony reached by a right-angled stone stairway, beneath it a wall and up there the guests—

the laughingly-occupied gentry, one could call them, as in Renaissance paintings of the subject—was just the place for an execution. The atmosphere was rich and stark.

We mounted the stairs and joined the throng, looked into a room to the left, crimson and phosphorescent with crucifixes, a case of silver chalices, a monstrance, candlesticks, on one wall an agonised saint, so that I took this to be the family chapel: but it was only a room with another balcony overlooking another courtyard, this time filled with plants and heated so that guests there could play bridge. She couldn't see her mother, so we came back, skirted the corridor of bedrooms, and descended a main stairway hung with armour and the rest of the wallspace filled with paintings, madonnas and filibustering angels and scenes of colonial clergy with Indians, all set in immense gilt frames carved in the Churrigueresque manner and decorated with tiny mirrors.

Facing us in the main hall of the house, among a profusion of cut flowers, were even more people, streaming in and out of the sitting and dining rooms to the right and, others entering by the front door from the main car-filled courtyard ahead, so that one could have thought it a first night at the opera if it hadn't been for the atmosphere, defiantly tough and self-conscious of power yet not without apprehension, more like a ball on the eve of Waterloo. There were quite a few uniforms. There was a priest. There was jewellery galore and satin sheen. There were men standing in groups or singly whom one recognised as expert swordsmen, not dressed for the part but ready in a flash, pride and malice blending with the smiles with which they meanwhile teased the women. It was the atmosphere of the Press again. This was one of the bastions at issue.

From the sitting room one looked out on a terrace and a lawn and a further garden, down the side of which and built above the wall that ran high and white around the property, was a new wing extending from the main entrance courtyard, from I was told, the old stables, and at the end of this they had built the ballroom, next to the pool, just short of the orchard. Her sister, Consuelo

Rose, nineteen and the baby of the family, was dance mad, and her parents preferred, turn and turn about with other parents, to keep this craze where they could keep an eye on it.

"The Father advised it," murmured Paula non-committally, as the lone priest approached to be greeted: a dark sensual intelligent man. On our course so far she had been hailed and hugged, her hand kissed, her appearance praised, and attentively each time she had introduced me, then swept me on as though it were unlikely I would bump into any of them again. One could see she came of arrogant stock. Yet at the same time with her little asides, her softly floating contemptuous air, she was treating me as a confederate. I'm showing you round the zoo, she seemed to say.

Her mother was approaching across the lawn, and that was Consuelo with her, glowingly dark in a sea of dark beauty, with lustrous shoulders and pearls and silk, and a champagne haze about her face, setting off the jet of her hair heaped in a high wig front. They both regarded Paula sceptically, as if they had decided she might not come, then all three laughed lightly; Consuelo spoke some words of English, and dashed off with attendant beaux, into another stream of compliments; Paula followed; I was left with the mother.

She was a wise salty-faced woman, used to the good life, with high square features and a definite voice, probing towards nice turns of phrase and interesting memories. She had spent half her youth in Paris, and now a part of each year in New York. She had the highest regard for England and the English, in London she visited the museums and theatres—"you see, Paula was bound to be an artist, the way we brought her up," she said. "You know, her husband, Luis Felipe, is half Scottish, on his mother's side. I do so wish more of your countrymen would settle in Peru. We need your ability to compromise." She looked me over, suit and shirt, English manner and faulty Spanish, as if none the less she would find me a post in the next government she helped to arrange. "Now let me introduce you to someone who is a passionate Anglophile."

On the way to do this she collected a gentleman who had served in the diplomatic service, who now lived in his villa in Chosica, a sunny hamlet in the nearby hills: one Oscar Germán de la Fuente Castro, as his briskly produced card proclaimed. I fortunately had name cards on me, and indeed in Peru these were to be as important as wearing a tie and trimming one's nails, and as we exchanged these he gave a flourish that made me feel I was at least a king. His ease of manner overpowered one. His voice was clear and modulated, dropping each word one by one into an ancient and heraldic pattern. These arrangements he presented to his hostess as if filling the air with salaams and kisses. He also seemed to think she had given him the job of looking after me.

So I soon found myself in a clump of gentlemen, all of them passionate Anglophiles. "I used to stay with Lord Q," one said; "wonderful countryside near Bath" He assumed I must know Lord Q. "They had a magnificent family place there. When he came out here I showed him around. Are you perhaps interested in architecture? There are still a few odd corners in Lima, and some remarkable collections—well, you see one here." He graciously included a showcase of pre-Columbian ceramics beside us, on top of which were cocktail glasses abandoned as at gallery previews. "I could take you back to other days—alas, only in prints, sir, in a few relics of the time. It is no longer the Lima of La Perricholi." This brought laughs of fellow feeling. "No," he insisted, with an actor's gravity, "it is no longer the Lima of Santa Rosa. We are decadent. We belong now to the twentieth century."

I should like to have taxed him on this point; but another gentleman, equally brisk, with the same glowing horsey complexion, was recalling Britain's part in the liberation of Latin America from the dominion of Spain. "Everyone today," he pontificated, "takes note of the help our countries receive from the United States of North America. But they forget Castlereagh, they forget Canning. They forget Lord Cochrane. The British Navy decided our freedom—and I'm glad to say that Peru still gets its naval vessels from Great Britain. I wish we saw more of the British influence. Don't forget, either, the Royal Society: not all the new notions came out of France, sir, just because they had a Revolution. Britain also had the new outlook: rational, abstract, optimistic!"

He paused, and indeed, though they all assented, with the good grace that was obligatory, the word "revolution", and those other words, calling up so much they disliked, gave them a single stoney stare as if they had retreated into a frieze. The Enlightenment for them was still an issue. They still moved with a part of themselves within the eighteenth century.

One said: "But what counts is Peru. A Peruvian solution! A national philosophy! We cannot take too much from outside. After all, it is an ancient country: we absorbed a great empire here."

I felt this was my cue; but before I could speak another gentleman had waved this aside, switching them into Spanish, with "it cracked before a handful of Spaniards! The mass of Indians were as brutish then, as sub-human, as they are now. I find this cult of the primitive absurd. We are sabotaged by it. It is a piece of folly. Let us stick to the civilised realities".

His tone though lavishly polite was peremptory; and the fire in his eye, the personal involvement, brooked no contradiction. The ex-diplomat was putting on expressions of "absolute agreement" and "remarkable insight" and "well played, sir, at last the truth!" The one who had spoken before smiled cynically, but backed down. It was a risky topic.

Another one said, "Perhaps criminal folly? For those who lecture us upon the Indian do so for their own advancement. Naturally, at our expense. Gentlemen, let us forget the subject. Our friend here must be mystified." He twinkled charm and refinement at me. A stoical upstanding figure, as against his companion's rather overfed bulk, he was the tallest man in the room and the nearest to one's idea of a Spanish knight. "Will you be staying a good season in Peru? Or is it just a quick business trip?"

I confessed, though I was sorry to offend their taboos, that not only was I a writer (their expressions at once changed this to "troublemaker"), but that it was precisely the Indian and his customs (and now I added, "and his role today") that had lured me in the first place. I hedged too late, "Though I'm beginning to see there is much of interest in Lima itself".

Their regard bit into me. Could I be serious? Should they arrange to have me deported? A troublemaker, a crypto-Communist? Hardly what they looked for from Britain.

But in an instant this suspicion had been replaced by a guarded sauve acquiescence. Like themselves I was a guest of the Montellanos. (I suppose their minds worked in this way.) Other English writers, one quite recently, had done the standard trip and lauded Peru. All Englishmen were eccentrics, but equally far too decent to say the wrong thing. And might I not mean the Amazonian Indian, the naked denizen of the jungle?

Asking me this, and hearing no, the tall gentleman persisted—"Please go to Iquitos! The most fascinating place in our country, and typical! Three-fifths of Peru is jungle, sir. You can hire a boat and native guides and explore the Amazon. What experience for a writer!"

My conscience allowed me to agree with this, and to ask how one got to Iquitos, and to listen to his own Amazon story; and then to the others' Amazon stories, till it was clear that to have an Amazon story was *de rigueur* among the Lima élite. But still, as it was clear my intention remained to go rather for the Andean Indian, the one they meant when they said "sub-human", they began now to talk among themselves. Best to have nothing more to do with it.

Excusing myself, I sloped off.

Señor de la Fuente, almost in tears, came after me, waving distress signals. What a diplomatic calamity! How unused I must be to polite society! Catching me up by another showcase of pre-Columbian ceramics, he urged, "Señor, allow me to direct your interest. Look, it is among beautiful things like these, from

the Mochica culture, and these from Nazca, and here, not quite
so pure, Chimu, that you will find the true soul of our country.
At my house you may handle such pieces by the hour. I will
conduct you, if you allow me the honour, through the National
Museum—no, I will take you where you yourself may purchase,
for a trifle" (he whisked a handkerchief out and flutteringly
dabbed his nose) "equally rare pieces for yourself. Like that"
(bow, scrape, kisses) "you will conserve a serene picture of your
travels."

"Too kind," I murmured. I turned back to the display, far too
dense as though it were a larder, of Mochica jugs in the shape of
birds, frogs, fish, or the human head, backed by the single stirrup
spout, and of polychrome Nazca bowls, and of double-spouted
Chimu ware, all handworked for they hadn't known the wheel,
but various and sometimes subtle in design and colouring and
decoration. "Were these made by sub-humans?"

"My dear Señor, I beg your pardon?"

A minute later he was saying, "Yes, may I be frank? You have
put your finger on a great problem. It is perhaps for history to
solve. For no one can deny this artistic quality; and yet, as I fear
you will see for yourself, the Indian is unredeemably brutish.
Despite all our efforts, he remains bestial, a Stone Age captive, a
New World Caliban. I cannot continue. Have you heard of
coca?"

"Coca Cola? Cocaine?"

He launched into a grim description of coca chewing among
the natives. It obviously distressed him greatly, so much so that he
had to finish it in French; but he recovered. We were edging
along the hall, and somehow out of the corner of his eye and with
one hand he greeted people, kisses for them, horror for me, until
we reached the front door. I believe he wanted to kick me through
it. But at that moment an acquaintance arrived, an American with
a Peruvian wife, who was immediately shouting about the
bullfight they had met at the previous Sunday—"Oh baby, that's
the spectacle in Lima!"—so that perforce he swept us inwards

together, and so back to the sitting room to a different corner and different people. Shortly afterwards he disappeared.

There was nothing I wanted less at this point than to continue the Indian polemic. Gradually, I felt, I might tease out the truth, but not on such an evening. Despite all, I was enjoying it here. I could feel myself growing into Lima, lapping up its creole charm. I mustn't, because I had an English conscience, become a sort of bogeyman. I was really looking about for Paula, but couldn't immediately see her.

In this mood, then, I began eating and drinking, supplied by near-invisible servants, and chatting first to the Peruvian wife and then, because she was an obvious draw with her hypocritical discreet smiles, to her and to two youngish men: one of them of the swordsman type, witty and suave and game for anything, and the other oozing importance and affront. I gathered he was well-connected, but little else for his wordy preambles were undercut by the other's thrusts. Beyond them the room might have been the scene of the South Sea Bubble before it burst: living it up, with determination not to heed adverse omens. In the distance, mambos; nearer to, the round game of salty compliments. Through them the evening's pace developed.

Alas, it was as if the canker in me mysteriously affected others, or else they were more anxious than appeared, for after a while, an enjoyable while, the shameful subject surfaced again. The pompous young man had referred to the budget, balanced at last, which he took as a signal for a new phase of industrial expansion. More factories, more jobs. He admitted to owning a factory himself. But where were they to find technicians, or anyone to be relied on? Peruvians—and he loaded his tone with contempt as if he had been a Chilean—were useless! Only good for strikes. There was too much Indian blood in the country, making for laziness and low intelligence. They must stop this drift of peasants to the cities. Import Italians, Hungarians! He would even rather see more Chinese.

"Bring in more Chinese," flashed the other, "and you'll find

Peru belonging to China! Already, on every Pacific island, there are Chinese colonies like stepping stones. But as for the native, our Indian peasant, I think we can deal with him, if need be." His smile grew wicked. "As we've done before."

"Oh don't mention natives to me! Dirty lying drunken creatures!" The Peruvian wife rattled this out, her flightiness taking on hard contours. "One can't drive out of Lima these days without seeing their filthy shacks. Why don't the police send them back to the hills? It's becoming a besieged city."

She turned to me: "The Government has offered good land in the east of Peru; but these creatures prefer to live off us. They live like pigs! I don't understand your English ladies, and French and Swiss ladies, who actually visit these slum quarters, these barriadas we call them, in the hope of changing the filthy creatures. I wouldn't do it with my last breath. You can imagine the promiscuity found there!"

Breath failed her, though she was also on the brink of scabrous revelations.

The swordsman flashed: "Fathers with daughters! Sons with each other, or animals! All in the one room together! And they are said to have television sets." He saw this was silly, and rescued himself—"We shall have to smoke them out eventually." He turned to me, "Animals!"

I didn't like any of this, their intensity alone was suffocating: I countered, "But isn't it to do with poverty, and a sort of hopelessness? It's the same in Cairo and Calcutta. It can all be solved, rationally."

A mild enough tone, but the swordsman flashed, cutting me into fifty pieces. Todo o nada. I was now an enemy. And the wife shrugged as though I had said something she had not heard properly. The pompous one parleyed a bit longer . . . "Señor, have you been here very long? Would you, if you had money to invest, entrust it to illiterate savages? We are trying to establish a modern society, based on power, steel, oil—in my own case, on low-priced textiles. We have the same right to this as you. That is our problem. One of priorities! Afterwards"... he was comprehensive, visionary . . . "in the future, then, we can attend to the peasants. Educate, begin ... on my own estate, I have tried a small pilot scheme, but I have not seen any results. Leave us to deal with what we understand, Señor." The anger in him was edging up.

"Certainly. I only arrived this afternoon. But what strikes me," I said with emphasis, as sword-sharp as I could make it, "is that everyone is discussing the Indian—or the native, or animal, or whatever you call him. And that you are all worried and hitting out blindly. For however ignorant a stranger is, he knows you have peasants and a feudal system, and that since Castro's rise in Cuba you can't get away with it much longer. Forgive my bluntness; but I'm beginning to see that this small point is immensely interesting. The Indian rules the situation, though he lives in shacks, and in remote valleys has to suffer being whipped. The rest is Limeñan political froth."

My God, I'd certainly done it now. Worse than not playing ball in a nut house, worse than stealing medals from a paranoiac. At least I would have a duel on my hands. I added, "After all, in Rhodesia we have had to come to terms with a similar truth. It's just a worldwide movement."

No good. They were deaf, murderously indifferent to anything beyond the frontiers of Peru. But here, in their own land . . . "Señor!"—it was the wife, elegant with poison, poised to slap back the insult—"as you are so well informed, I believe also that you have a political interest in this matter?"

"Oh, if anything, I'm a Conservative," I said.

It is strange to be hated so soon for so little.

Paula rescued me. I could feel her hand on my arm, and I saw she had the gist of the scene. "Come and meet my father"; and she smiled at the trio as though they had been so kind to amuse me. "I hope your studies are progressing," she murmured.

We left the room by another door, and followed stairs that became a bridge above the garden end of the courtyard, so that we could see the cars and chauffeurs on the one side, and the firefly throng of guests on the lawn crossing between the house and the ballroom; and beyond the wall that ran around the property was an olive grove and, surprisingly near, other residences, and roads; and somewhere in the locality the sky reflected the flash of a neon sign. Ahead, above the old stables, her father had his study.

"Esteban Montellano, my father." She had said it as if she were introducing the performer she loved best of all.

He had the same jowl, a big man, thick; he came towards you like a boxer from his corner, his eyes aware of you two moves ahead; then as his voice broke, rippling at speed, his face became all quips and humour. He embraced you with a handshake. Cigar? Whisky? Sit in this chair, low, and cut in black leather. Of course, you'd already noticed the Cézanne, and up there the Braque, the Picasso, bought just before the boom in New York. Trifles. Come and look out of this window, down there against the white wall. See? Perfect, a perfect stone head, from Chavín de Huantar. Throw the rest away.

Now what was your line of country?

"Look after him," he said to Paula finally.

I knew at that moment I was launched.

The sequel came when I broached an idea beginning to turn round in my head, that I needed a base in Lima, in a family—somewhere very unpretentious, for preference—and she nodded agreeably, with such a different kind of face from the immobile gloom she had first presented, and said, "Well, it's not so usual. A sort of pension, no? You mean, a family? Peruvians tend to build walls between their family life and the outside world. We live in our clans like fish in an aquarium. But, as it so happens, I have an idea. I'd better first ask my mother."

She added, "It concerns one of our cousins, a widow, with children, who does accept occasional students. If they are particularly recommended. She can do with the money. Now she"...
and Paula became animated . . . "is an extraordinarily brave and

interesting woman. Her husband was a cholo—oh, there's quite a story! Some people call it . . . our family skeleton." She grinned, realising how it all fell together. "I say, I am helping on your studies!"

"I'll ring you first thing in the morning," she promised. "At your hotel."

2

A BASE IN LIMA

THE phone rang early and by ten past nine she had collected me at my hotel. She drove a Volkswagen, wore a dark brown suit with rather severe cut of blouse, and was pleasant but briskly impersonal. "I'm sorry to do things at such a rush, but I'm leaving Lima before lunch. I thought I'd better see you installed. I hope in the last hour our Señora hasn't changed her mind." Her eyes lit up with the pranks she was playing, but the impulse was fading, her mouth moved with the beginnings of impatience.

I thanked her for the previous evening, asking if she had been born in that house.

"No, I was born in Arequipa, at my grandfather's house. We were already in Lima, but it was easier for my mother. We acquired that house just after the war. Before, we lived nearer the sea."

"Do you mean our war?"

She smiled faintly. "I admit it was remote. Everything is remote from behind the Andes. People fondly imagine it will save us when the hydrogen bombs start flying." She shrugged. "Does it matter?"

"Arequipa is to the south, isn't it? Is that why you and your father, for instance, have rather particular features?"

"Do we?" She looked her most sceptical. "Oh . . . not more than other Arequipeñans, and you spoke to quite a few last night. Yes, it is to the very south; and it used to be distinctive: very traditional, very Spanish. It claimed to give Peru its moral fervour, and, periodically, its saviour. It's rather a sad spot now, though."

"Pure Spanish?"

34

"My dear Señor, what does one ever mean by pure? Are the English pure? Are the Dutch pure? My family alone mixes Roman energy with Iberian temper, Moorish dreams, Indian tenacity—and, somewhere, an Irishman joined us! Still, in one respect, with regard to the Indians, after the first orgy on arrival, we didn't mix for four hundred years, until, and I began to tell you last night, until the Señora you are now to meet, Señora Echarri, married a doctor who was distinctly more Indian than Spanish."

"A mestizo?"

"Well, yes. We don't use the word. Say cholo—though, as you'll discover, there are as many ways of saying it as there are of saying Yankee."

She paused, perhaps feeling she was talking too much: the effect of driving, or of finding herself doing someone such a good turn. Her expression turned a shade moodier.

But, she was halfway through and she wanted to finish. We were already out on Avenida Arequipa, the collectivo run of the night before, and she had warned there wasn't far to go.

"So," she deliberated . . . "she would never have been able to marry him down in Arequipa, in that small cathedral town atmosphere; her mother in any case was all against it. So she came up here. He was just returning from the States. My parents were already well established in Lima—ahead, at that time, of the mass migration—and they helped. Carmen Maria and my mother had been school friends . . ." She paused. "I too remember him. He could have become Peru's best doctor. But he died; leaving five children behind him. Now you begin to understand? I'm not going to tell you more."

She shut up with an admonitory sharpness, and swung into a transverse street, then slowed for two turnings. "Remember," she said, "it's room and breakfast. Anything more would embarrass the family. Especially at midday—it's then they're together."

She drew up before a narrow frontage of grey stucco, in bad repair. There was a garage built into one side of it, but the door was dusty and trailing with briars from a pergola that, like the foot of front garden, was more a gesture than anything else. To the left were linked two similar houses, one of them with a new coat of paint, and then what could be an apartment house, four storeys high and also gloomy, ending in a row of shops and a café. To the right was a house then a high blank wall as far as the next corner; opposite, similar houses, and an area of demolition across part of which ran a new street, rubble, and at the tip a block of flats of about ten storeys, topped by an airline advert. Traffic raced a street away, and there could be seen one wing of a large building that Paula indicated as the hospital where Doctor Echarri had worked. It was a nondescript transitional district.

A pregnant maid opened the door. It was a dull morning and the hall was dark, and it was not much lighter in the sitting room, small, and made smaller by the surrounding wall furniture. A central table sang with polish but the settee looked dusty. There were shelves of books—I remarked these, because I had seen none at the Montellanos'—a case cluttered with Victorian china, oleographs of the Madonna and Child and a print of an Alpine valley, a writing desk that looked to have been left as last used several years before, and an array of framed photographs. Among these, of children growing up, in school uniforms, and being confirmed, it was easy to pick out the doctor: a dark face with still darker eye sockets, rugged and vehemently high-minded.

The Señora had entered. A smallish woman, round-shouldered in a thick wool cardigan, her walk was determined but her high white face worn with cares and advancing age. She looked flustered, a trifle vexed, but her greeting was soft-spoken and exploratory. It struck me she didn't like Paula and this made me feel uncomfortable. Their glances sheered off to the furniture. She pinpointed me with a single look, not unkind but totally uninterested. There was a pause as if nothing really had been fixed.

Then Paula abruptly excused herself. My luggage, after all, had been taken by the maid. I was in. There was nothing more she could do. Her tall, very expensive presence removed itself with

barely a wave, and the gears grinded as she sped away. The dusty
silence settled down.

"Let me show you your room," said the Señora. We mounted
to the next floor and to a room overlooking the street. It was a
small meticulously clean room, the bare boards swept and polished,
the bedside carpet beaten thin. There was a crucifix above the
bed, lace edgings to the sheets, a wardrobe. On one wall, above a
wicker table, was a disconcertingly sexy calendar. The maid at
this moment appeared with my suitcase.

"Señora Alvano," said the Señora, in her soft slightly challeng-
ing voice, "told me that you were a student?"

"Ah yes?" I knew I mustn't explain the jest; it would be un-
acceptable to her. So I said I was studying colonial history: an
alibi, it flashed through my mind, innocuous enough for the night
before. Her fretful face made no comment.

"Fernando!" She called to a figure slipping past the door. A
young man materialised, unshaven, poorly dressed. She introduced him as Señor Olivero, studying to be an industrial chemist.
He was polite, shy, and in his shadowy glances almost as uncertain as she was. I could feel this household had been discussing
my coming, in the short space Paula had given them, and taking
a doubting vote upon it. The maid was gobbling me up, watching
to see what would happen next.

The Señora dismissed her, and said, "Forgive me, but Peru has
too many young people who wish to study history and law. It
is a way of being gentlemen. We need more to follow Fernando."

I agreed warmly, but with a whispered "Señor," Fernando had
slipped away.

The Señora mused, showed me the bathroom, mentioned the
price for room and breakfast, and said that at whatever hour I
returned the maid, Meche, would let me in. She did not refer to
my meeting her children or to use of the sitting room: I could
feel her consciously drawing a line. "I hope you will be comfortable," she murmured politely, but in effect she had not accepted
my presence.

Then I was sitting alone in my room.

I did the usual things, to feel more at home: tried the bed, unpacked, set out my photos. What a beginning! Was it going to be hopeless? I gave the bathroom a closer look, sniffed at a variety of expensive lotions in contrast to the austerity elsewhere, and returned to my room, my allowed domain. I pulled out a map of the city. Well, now I had to set off for the day and not return too awkwardly soon. But despite this, despite all, I felt differently inside Lima.

On the stairs going down I rubbed past Meche, humming and staring into space. The rest of the house was like a grave.

I went first to the corner café, bought a paper from a ragged infant, surrendered my shoes to a shoeshine boy, and ordered a ham sandwich and coffee. The day now was starting afresh. To have a room and to go to one's café was more like being a person somewhere—the café as important as the room. This place looked congenial. The name above the door was Chong, and the young girl serving was a rapturous mixture of Negro Indian Spanish Chinese: perhaps mostly Chinese, for the floor was spotless, and the plates, and the till rattled like an abacus, but then the samba from the radio seemed to suit her and she had long smooth black hair. She slightly evoked Tahitian girls.

The coffee however was undrinkable: a thick black syrup to which one could add, from jugs provided, either hot milk or hot water. But the Chinese tea with lemon was good.

From a window table I watched the street, cars and itinerant vendors and idlers, and what took shape as the neighbourhood: at this hour the wives and maids shopping and doing errands and returning to this or that door to gossip. The tailor's and the cobbler's shop, minute dark doorways, were great centres of collision, and between these, a strategic point, the ragged newspaper infant, supplied I could see from a kiosk at the corner, began hawking magazines. An empty school bus passed. A uniformed schoolgirl, abysmally late, trailed along the pavement. There was a beggar, as though pushed up from the drains, only half of him as yet above the ground, one arm feebly pleading. A policeman passed, an idle-looking youth. There were fat matrons, thin matrons, pleated skirts and white gloves swishing by en route to the bus stop, trousers and sandals slopping about. Some minute before ten a bell tolled and an old woman in black appeared. The first smells of the midday meal filtered into the air.

A tolerant unobtrusive neighbourhood, just about making ends meet. And on all sides, the city extending.

I caught a bus, a street away, and began a cheap circular tour. Almost at once the district improved, with villas, maids in uniform, trees; we crossed an imposing avenue thronging with a different species of car; and then, past some dizzying flats and more villas, back to the semi-decay and demolitions, this time running into factories and bus yards and wide commercial-looking thoroughfares. Down one of these I caught a collectivo, but almost at once there were villas again, the district once again improving, and now I could feel the sea approaching, the patchy plaster and the bougainvillaea and the washing fluttering on rooftops suggesting some corner of Nice or Alexandria, so that for a moment one could ask if the Greeks and Phoenicians hadn't established this coast too: but of course the Spaniards within them carried the entire story of the Mediterranean. And in this collectivo, on this cheaper run, the passengers were arguing ten to the dozen, and a woman was giving her child the breast. Arguing vociferously, with that soft politeness.

The sea was a thin grey line of water below the mist three hundred feet below the cliff top balustrade. To the north the sun was glimmering through. Not a day to see the Pacific. And the rest of it, along this front, which I journeyed by continuing collectivo, was fencing, rubble, rubbish lots, a few immense villa walls, and the mist clammily over everything.

At Miraflores I had a nip of cognac and passed the Rodas' front door: they already seemed a world away. I caught an Avenida Arequipa collectivo, and inevitably with it the stiff-comporting company experienced on the previous evening: the same white collars and shot cuffs, knife-edge creases, trimmed moustaches, the women silky-looking (whatever they were wearing), and all the expressions gravely involved with problems, perhaps of bridge or behaviour, and much of it one guessed to do with money.

At this hour it was a fast run: barely eight minutes to my new district (the hospital looming a block away), and a further five to San Martin. Back to yesterday, but how different it felt to be looking at Lima from the inside! Well, that was still an exaggeration: for already a lunchtime queue was forming for the collectivos coming in, to take people home to their families, and possibly the Señora's sons and daughters were in it, how could one know, and gathered at table they might finally decide against taking the stranger: whilst I in the meantime had to go back to yesterday's streets and cafés. I began to feel I needed that family, must stick to it, become a part of it.

I am sure all travel is a shaking up: one suddenly can't take anything for granted. Friends, conversation, domestic trifles, familiarity with a wall or a tree: everything has to be built from scratch. This certainly improves one's manners; though perhaps not one's character.

I entered a bookshop and asked for a novel by any of Peru's younger writers that dealt with peasant conditions in the Andes. After being offered a number of books that seemed rather to deal with tramps and homosexuals in the city slums and prisons (as with the painters, interest had shifted from the somewhat over-worked Indian), I fastened on Pedro Azuarga, whose work, I was assured, was dense and cruel, highly political, and thoroughly sound. Thus recommended, for a mere ten soles (approximately half a crown), I bought the first novel he had written, a decade before, and set off for lunch. The bookseller told me where to go.

The restaurant was Raimondi's, to become a favourite haunt of mine, once again bordered by a sewer-like street packed with foul fumes, but pleasantly staid within and smelling only of tempting kinds of food. The waiter chose—an opening mouthful of highly spiced shellfish chowder, then corvina, a kind of sea bass, with fresh beans and salad, then cheese, and with all this a local wine, and afterwards an excellent coffee. Optimism flooded

back; and, reading the news and a bit of the novel, zeal to go off
to the Andes returned—I mean, could such horrible events be
true? The decade seemed to have been for the worse; but firstly
I must win over the Señora, secure the base, and fit in there. To
think about her was to like her more, to see past her initial
vexation. And consider, she had been born Carmen Maria
Montellano y Peñas of Arequipa, of a seigniorial family, and she
had married a cholo (whatever that word exactly meant), a
brown-faced doctor, one Señor Echarri; she had children growing up with this mixture within them, and the most cursory
glance around one now, or in the street or collectivo showed,
though perhaps at more ordinary social levels, such mixtures to
be the stuff of Peru. As in God's eyes they were bound to be.

A major reason for respecting the Señora. Caste had not stood
in the way.

The afternoon dragged terribly. I was so impatient to be
back in that house. I couldn't face a church or museum, or the
frenzied traffic, or the town centre; I nipped back to the neighbourhood, more personal at least, and drank tea. At five I rang
the front door bell.

The maid answered. She was nine months gone, at least, but
unconcerned. I could hear a child whining in the background.
"Is that your little boy, too?" I enquired; it was such a pleasure to
be talking again. It was her child, and I babbled "Like mine,"
and she cried, "Si, Señor, what beautiful photos!", and we both
knew she had been inspecting my belongings, and I didn't mind,
and felt more at home. Some minutes later she knocked on the
door, "Señor, do you have any washing for me?" As I hesitated
she calmly said, "You will want to change your shirt for evening.
I will wash it together with Señor Roberto's." I complied, and
as she took it I asked, "So what is your little boy's name, Meche?"
"Jesús," she cried, and laughed simply.

She looked back, laughing, as she went down the stairs.

It was then I noticed a young gentleman watching. He had a
taut disapproving face: and I felt it, for it implied I had been
flirting with the maid, which was untrue: but he stepped

forward, lean, swarthy, a young version of the swordsman type, with the clear intention of reproving me.

"Señor!" He flashed a card. Roberto Juan Echarri Montellano. "It is a great honour to make your acquaintance." He was aloof, contemptuous, yet in some way already insinuating flattery and service.

I invited him into my room and he accepted, and accepted a cigarette, and then, with a slightly disagreeable smile that hovered on the very tips of his moustache, "It is inadvisable to encourage the girl, Señor. It is not just her condition, but her especial failing. The father, this time, is a local policeman. My mother is too good-hearted to her."

I assured him I should never encourage the maid; but he waved this aside, as if the point had been settled by his own mention of it; then he continued on the subject of Meche's failings. A simple girl, a sad story; she had followed her first "husband" to Lima— "we call them husbands out of politeness"—but had found him living with another girl, another "conviviente". So she'd looked for work; but her first employer, an officer, had thrown the soup in her face and another day had knocked her to the ground. At that time she had been expecting Jesús.

Señor Roberto smiled faintly. "I would not put it past her mentality to have been expecting Him literally! You know, she is only fifteen."

He continued, "My mother took her in, as she comes from a village of our province. It is necessary to protect such creatures in Lima. As you see, we do not entirely succeed." He was savouring the story, mixing his contempt with a certain lustful satisfaction. I suddenly saw he was confiding in me. I began to pay more heed to his warnings.

These swordsmen were touchy people.

Anyway it had served to get us talking, and next as I let him establish, as he wished to, that I had the ear of the Montellanos, with Paula no more than a go-between (like his mother he appeared strongly to resent her), he became interested in my company. His expression softened, to show respect, indolence, all the favours he would be able to do for me; and it also let through quite a pressure of greed. We went out round the corner to a bar, with some name like Capri and a juke box. He allowed me to pay, for the excellent lager, but not without a dark flush of reproof. In the better light I could see better the mobility of his features. Whether this reflected his innermost soul or simply the play of an actor's talent, I couldn't know; and if he had been purely white he would have bored me, with his little affronts and self-esteem, and hair that explained those bathroom lotions: but he had a skin colour of medium chestnut, slightly greyed over. He was mestizo. It was different.

It was if we were three people talking.

He suddenly decided to pay for a beer. He launched into a further confidence. Then, on the way home, regretted doing it.

So that was my first encounter with Roberto, aged twenty, engineering student. Keen? Yes. Peru required him. His father had wished it. It was his destiny. Well, perhaps, sometimes not. He was not too keen on leaving Lima. Not keen, as he put it, on burdening his mother. It might be sounder to switch to law.

There were imponderables. He dismissed my interest.

But when we arrived back at the house, the door of which he opened with his key, he waved me into the sitting room. His mother was there, a bit hunched, chilled, for there was no heating in evidence, and her eyes smiled, tired and thoughtful, but with unconscious relief as she saw him enter. She gradually extended the welcome, and then asked me to sit down.

"Señor." She was offering tea, biscuits. There were still reservations, but pushed away temporarily. She asked me a few family questions, then remarked on my coming alone to Peru. I explained that, and she looked more at ease. A niche was being constructed for the stranger. She began suddenly to talk about a strike of school teachers that was a week old. Her married daughter, Juanita, had formerly been a school teacher. It was essential they stood firm this time. Her voice rose with nervous clarity.

Roberto looked bored, and paid her a compliment. She put

her arm against him, but continued talking, Her white face and
mental calibre were in sharp contrast to his; did she pity him?
She appeared to idolise her son; but equally, involved with a
question of principle, she brushed his playfulness aside and thrust
on determinedly. He wandered about and tried the radio, and
left it playing when he went upstairs; but nothing now deterred the
Señora, who had strong views on the social order, so that within
her voice one could hear the trumpets blown through a lifetime
of test and challenge, if muted slightly by good manners. Behind
her, on a shelf, stood a photo of her husband: still inspiring her,
still learning from her. She must have been like this as a girl.

"You are studying colonial history? Señor, look at Peru
today. Is it not still a colony?"

She was suddenly tired. I stood up to go. Her eyes bore into me
thoughtfully, a little anxiously again, I thought. "If you have
time," she pondered slowly, "my daughter would be happy to
receive you tomorrow. I spend most evenings there. I hope,
Señor, you are not offended by my rather outspoken opinions?"

"I, Señora? I am very ignorant. But a radical to the fingertips."

"Good!" She was delighted, and surprised. Her reservations
seemed to lift.

"Good," she repeated, "my daughter will be pleased." She
gave me the first real smile of welcome.

At the door I paused, "Excuse me, Señora, but I understood
you had five children?"

"One is dead." Her voice was hesitant. "One, José, is in the
States. One you have met. One is Juanita. And Carmela is always
out at parties." She had ended again by smiling gently.

She rose, a sturdy little figure, her face keen beneath its sadness. "Sleep well, Señor. We will see you at breakfast. It is from
eight o'clock, in this room."

After that, of course, and her understanding smile, I slept as
with the angels.

Next day I stayed in the neighbourhood. Awake at six I heard
the milk delivered, and, looking out, saw a trail of maids bringing

fresh bread home. It was easy to get into the bathroom, and by the time I was down the lower part of the house had been cleaned, the table set, and some shopping done for the midday meal. Meche looked sleepy-eyed, but the Señora as if she had been up since five, quietly, methodically constructing the day. It was she who attended to my breakfast—Fruit? Cornflakes? Tea or coffee? An egg? She presented the list with a certain whimsicality, for it was clearly outside her usual routine; when the others came down they called to Meche, and were given coffee, then helped themselves to the bread and white cheese on the table. Roberto made a point of wanting toast. Neither he nor Fernando rose to conversation.

Then in came a girl, of whitish complexion, say white with a good ski-ing tan, vivaciously dressed but not quite so young as that and her make-up tried to convey, about to explode with bad temper until she noticed there was a stranger present. Her greeting was easily controlled, her eyes lighting up with automatic smiles. This was Carmela, small and dainty, swinging as she walked, her vigour striking out through the tap of her heels and the flick of her fingers, so that the next stage would have been flamenco: but now stopped short by her mother's reproof, "How could you be back so late? I fell asleep waiting up for you!" There followed an exchange as to the exact time at which Carmela had come home, cut by the girl, after a sip of coffee, excusing herself as being late for the office. Obstinate and neat, and already turning with the excitements of a new day, she fled the house.

It was a slightly more sunny morning, but not so as one could see the sky. A sweater was needed to keep warm. I fell into talk at the newspaper kiosk, after a glance at the morning's headlines; who, I asked, was going to save the country? No one, he answered, nothing could be done. Best to shut one's eyes to politics, and simply try and get enough to eat. Money ruled, and one couldn't fight money. "La plata hace," he kept repeating, with sour philosophy, huddled in his kiosk—then, with sudden vehemence, striking at a paper that headlined new violence in the mountains,

"I could tell you stories! Cruel things I've seen with my own eyes. Men killed and their women driven to work for a harsh master. Do you think our laws allow that? Our written laws are models of their kind! Ah, but that's a different matter," he subsided, ironically; "and who is going to point a finger? People in this street cheat each other, and the cobbler whips his sons on Sunday." He tucked himself away beneath his coat, despising the world. Nothing further to say.

Over two crossings the lanes of traffic passed up and down Avenida Arequipa. Five minutes in the other direction was the traffic of Avenida General Salaverry. The hospital formed another wall, and on the other side, after some streets, the main avenues converged. This was the district, part of it decaying, part of it being built up anew. It contained two small shopping centres, a gasoline station, a cinema; and a small quadrangle of grass, mysteriously overlooked by developers, where students and children could pass their time. Actually the students, on strike, as I had learned, in sympathy with the schoolmasters, paradoxically looked very studious: an earnest group sharing a textbook and chalking their calculations on the pavement. One of them was learning a piece by heart, clutching a mimographed hand-out, pacing to and fro. But half an hour later this had broken up, they were exhausted; they began arguing nervously.

I might add that, to European eyes, they appeared less to belong to today's young people than to the generation of the Gorki films. They lacked the uniforms (I doubt they could have afforded them), but their pale stubbled dissatisfied faces and thin figures already gave them a sad maturity, an underdog look and restiveness betokening the pre-revolutionary scene. And again and again while travelling in Peru (though this anticipates the following pages) I was reminded not so much of descriptions of France before 1789 as of Russia before the twentieth century. Everywhere stalked Turgeniev's students, fiery and apathetic by turns, bearing the cross of things to come.

By contrast the café was modestly affluent, with a side trade in delicatessen, and soups and omelettes and cold cuts for a company of drivers and mechanics, and small men of affairs, husbands having an extra snack, and the district's professional idlers. It hummed through most hours of the day. Occasionally a woman came in with a man, but no woman sat down alone.

Evening came round rather quickly. I had finished Azuarga's book—my words, fresh fuel for the course I was on—causing me to notice, however dark they were, that none of my neighbours conversed in Quechua, the Indian speech, very likely, of their parents left behind in the hinderland: all spoke Spanish, all wore suits or jeans, check shirts, leather jackets. There was quite an admixture of negro blood, adding a light sporty facility to topics under discussion. Football, boxing, the cost of living, the un-reliability of APRA, came up again and again.

From the papers I was getting a first glimmering of the nature of the political scene: the main parties in power and opposition, the elections eight months ahead that promised to be crucial for modern Peru, the hot issues, the unspoken realities; but it was pretty tangled at this stage. Why for instance did people from the Left, and others from the extreme Right, equally condemn APRA? All the parties received brickbats, but APRA was dodging them from every quarter.

But this was only one of many riddles.

The Señora, over her thick wool cardigan, wore a silk scarf and a coat. Other women in the bus wore suits or simply cardigans or twin sets. It was not a chilly evening. The mist had receded. We crossed Avenida Salaverry and got down just before Avenida Brasil, in that companion area of semi-decay I had passed through the previous morning. Here, on the first floor off a courtyard, the lower rooms rented by other families, lived her daughter Juanita, with husband and child, and another child expected about a month after Meche's. The husband, Emilio, was a professor of agronomy, a good man, a good father. The Señora, perhaps as each time she came here, took fresh heart as she climbed the stairs.

It was Juanita who opened the door, Juanita with a big pan of a face, moist and glowing with the beauty of life, her stomach pushing out in front. She was taller than her brother or sister, sallow-skinned with thick features, hair brushed back, large pools of eyes. She exuded an amiably-restrained ardour, that kept bursting out in a laugh or a remark that seemed to go to the heart of things. Otherwise she was brooding with small anxieties, tiny thoughts like clouds that went skimming across her countenance. As she spoke to you, she was most serene.

They were crushed in these two rooms, with a kitchen off, the space, as at her mother's house, and more remotely as at the Montellano mansion, made to seem smaller by the amount of furniture and bric-à-brac around the walls. There seemed to be so many upright chairs, and here again a cabinet of china, and a Madonna and Child; but, beside these, a Renoir print, a tall conical straw hat, panpipes, which came, I learned, from Cuzco, as many potted plants as photos, and then a single immense photo mounted on board that filled half a wall, that showed the high Andean plateau with scaly peaks rising at the side and in the middle distance a herd of cattle and herdsmen, dots in the grey desolation. No scheme to the room, but an accumulation of gifts, interests, souvenirs. Books were heaped on the floor in a corner, and others on a table with papers and a typewriter; a light on one wall wasn't working; a half-open door to the bedroom showed a comparable confusion there; and at the main table in the living room were a group of people who in posture and dress looked to have been equally casually added by this household's, perhaps by Juanita's, all-embracing abundant nature.

The husband came out from the bedroom, a dark alert very quiet man, carrying some photos to show his guests. He turned to us. Emilio Brozas. His handshake offered immediate friendship. He bore one along into a chair. Introductions were made, and then as if one were already a part of the talk in progress, he continued his points, showing the photos—look there, Señor Sykes, at the children's faces. In a new rural school. Explicit, no?— and before one could get sufficient grasp to ask a single intelligent question, the conversation had swept elsewhere. Two of the group were medical students. Another man was a fellow

agronomist. They had swept by way of the teachers' strike to a
tilt at the reigning Prado government, to the question of the
universities, before I could catch up with them. Juanita had set a
glass of wine beside me. She and her mother were sitting to one
side talking in short excited tones.

"The point is," said one of the students, "we can't trust anybody. The Government, that is, the ruling class, only wants a
few quality students, a top layer of technicians and specialists.
Too many of us are dangerous cattle. Hence it starves our every
need. Have you seen conditions at Cuzco university? At Arequipa?
Here at San Marcos? The student feels degraded by it. And our
professors, whatever they felt when young, now equally 'uphold
tradition'—that's half our trouble on the administrative councils
—and as often as not they don't give their lectures, they're so busy
with their private practices, or jobs on newspapers or in government offices. They are ratés—"

"Perhaps," said Brozas, with a sudden sly twinkle of humour;
"but what about those who stand by you, who understandingly
help with strikes, the agents provocateurs who use you—?"

"Oh sir, no." The student was pale. "We are front line troops.
We test the situation until the workers and peasants join us. We
need—"

"You said you couldn't trust anybody."

"Sir, we can trust you." There was laughter. Brozas held up a
finger, chipped in: "However we feel about some professors,
there is also the unworthy student, the 'comechado' of some future
office, who angles or bribes for a pass mark, who—"

"Sir, but who takes the bribes? And what about the 'great'
professors who have never been known to fail anyone!—"

Brozas nodded quickly, continued—"who is only too glad to
take to the streets. What about that kind of student? And those
who fight among themselves, as if at eighteen or twenty they
could know so precisely the difference between slogans?"

"Oh, sir."

"Well, think. Wouldn't it be wiser to work harder, and
leave politics alone? To become as fully equipped as you can, as

soon as you can, and then begin? We are going to rule the country, don't worry, we shall take it over: but we can't use half-trained technicians, rubber stamp lawyers and accountants, duds. Your part is to study, and watch. Later . . ."

"But then we shall be too old!"

"It is all a matter of money. Finance," interjected the other agronomist. "At San Marcos, for instance, each student pays ten dollars a year; and costs one hundred and eighty dollars; and on minimum standards ought to cost three hundred and fifty dollars. I think students should pay more, and certainly the Government on a regular, a permanent—"

"But that is what I said to start with!" The student was rising, his face agitated. Everyone stared at him now. He was clean-shaven, cleanly dressed, obviously blessed with adequate means; and later he might be found with the rich and powerful, those who had studied in the States or Europe, and intellectualise as they did; none the less for the moment he was here, ardent, self-respecting. His colleagues should appreciate, listen . . .

Brozas with his quiet authority waved him down. "My dear Correa, we shall change the government. By vote, through the growing power of morality. We no more need your demonstrations than we do the antics of palace dictators. All that era has been superseded, by technology and by world opinions. Look, our friend here is an Englishman, listening, and behind him are millions of listeners, and watchers, in Africa, Asia, Europe, even the United States, attentive to what happens in Peru. That is simply the modern world. That is why we shall change the government. That is why progress here is inevitable."

"I think rather, sir, if you will pardon my views, that just Castro listening and watching is more effective."

There were smiles, and as Brozas joined in, immediately accepting a new turn in the discussion, they all started to speak at once. But Juanita leaned over us, bearing a bowl of soup. "This evening," she said, "I have something special," and she and her mother served us with bread and a tasty sopa a la criolla, spiced with noodles and pieces of chicken. There were appreciative eating noises. Jokes. Brozas told an amusing experience. The argument came to a rest.

But not for long. They came here to debate, to test out their developing thoughts. Brozas was clearly someone they trusted. He was a man of absolute integrity.

Juanita and her mother were prattling away, and it was nice to see the Señora relaxed, enveloped by the pregnancy, and hear her tone of cautious pleading, "go more to Mass", and Juanita's reply, "Mamma, I don't have patience any more", and the *non sequitur* tick of seconds, then sighs and "Carmela comes home too late", and "Mamma, that girl makes you ill", and then the Señora, "And Roberto too. I don't know where that story will end": but all cradled by warmth and satisfaction as with purring cats beside the fire.

The Señora beckoned me to join them, and Juanita, with her caressing gaze and the gentle frankness of her condition, in a minute had extracted from me how I came to be sitting in her room, right back to the phone call to Infantes. "But that was only two days ago!" I was frightened the Señora might be annoyed. I said, "It already feels like a week." They laughed together, and complimented me on being "vivo", like all Limeñans—"our especial climate obviously suits you"; so I said, "Actually, what I want to do now is to take a first look at the sierra, to see how people live up there."

"Any particular place in mind?"

"No. A sort of first reconnoitre." I hadn't of course explained to them my growing interest in peasant conditions, or in the mixture of race in Peru.

Juanita said, "Your luck is holding. Emilio at the weekend has to go to Ayacucho, and he is going first to Huancayo, so as to see his uncle there. They are very strong APRA supporters— Apristas; though not Emilio any more. He'll tell you. It's a terrible story. At Ayacucho he has to do a survey for Huamanga University. I think you ought to go with him."

She called him. He eyed me carefully, as on journeys one often tells a great deal. One has to be sure of the other man.

Then he suspended judgment, perhaps out of politeness, and left it to his wife to fix the details. Her family seemed to have accepted me. (And this all the time was how it went in Peru.) And it was arranged that two days later, on Saturday, I should take the train up to Huancayo, and meet her husband there on the Sunday. He would have bought the bus seats onwards. "Take your warmest clothing. It might snow there at night." Then she and her mother turned back compulsively to further languorous maternal details.

The students were again in full swing; and the other one, quiet before, was now rapping his views on the table top. Beltran, Belaunde, Chavez, Odria, Haya de la Torre, the MSP, the PSP, APRA Rebelde: these were names of political leaders, and initials of splinter left-wing groups, and the argument concerned the electoral statute and how this framed each party's chances. It was as yet still beyond me. It seemed well argued, but it was like listening, by one who has never seen a bullfight, to aficionados weighing the chances of the bulls and their favourite matadors on the eve of the season's major contest.

"Don't be put off," said Brozas, "by those who tell you, and many will try to tell you this, that Peruvian politics are too confused for anyone else to understand. This is simply dust in the eyes. Motivations are not too obscure, even among us. One thing: up in the sierra everything becomes clearer. I'll see you there."

He walked with us down the street and saw us safely on to the bus.

We returned to the silent austere house.

The Señora began her nightly vigil, until Carmela should come home.

3

INLAND TO AYACUCHO

ROUND the Greek coast if there's the slightest wind the country-men lament the fate that sends them on a journey, and no sooner aboard the boats, the caiques, than they squat or lie flat in the scuppers, lemons to their mouths, prepared to be sick.

Similarly, among those on the train climbing from Lima to the central highlands, from sea level to a high pass of just under sixteen thousand feet, the thought of it alone, filled out no doubt by all those relations seeing them off, was enough to give to certain faces an uneasy film of green. As we left the cotton and sugar fields and climbed through orchards to the barren rock, and the air became sharper and the train tacked steeply up the canyon side in a series of switchbacks, the word siroche, meaning mountain sickness, rose clear out of conversations, and any clothing round the neck was loosed and determined sufferers prepared to suffer. To cap all, an attendant in white appeared with an oxygen bag, gas from which he was ready to offer to all our noses in turn; and this with perhaps its promise of survival, was the signal that set the prepared ones off. A woman gasped, clutched her forehead, then retched violently into a paper bag; another lolled back in her seat as if in the throes of the big dipper; whilst another plugged the blood from her nostrils. Everyone else continued as before, for though the atmosphere became a little thick it was no more so than in a nightclub.

At last we were entering the high plateau, the pampa or puna, as it was called, after a long morning up the gorges, a rather dim uphill journey, the cactus thinning till there had only been slate and vertical cliffs of grey-white rock winding between sun and shadow. We had stopped (on time, as it was a British-owned railway) at a miserable string of mining settlements. But, over the divide, the horizon widened, and though the sky thickened with cloud there was still sun on the snow peaks, reflected in a score of racing streams that cut the thin brown landscape. The horizon shot out ahead of us and there we were on top of the world.

Facing me across the window table was another Englishman; so after the usual uncertain beginnings we had talked, and he was an engineer of one of the big mining companies, and his Peruvian wife was forced each year to go down to Lima when the rains started. He had just been conducting her there, to her mother. His whole manner was a quiet celebration, and also his speech was soft and running and as if smoothed by lessons in the local Spanish, contrasting with his old grey flannels and sports jacket. He advised me while staying at the higher altitudes not to eat or drink much at night, so as to be able to sleep easily; and then he was explaining about the mines and their need to improve technical skills, to raise production with fewer miners. "Not like the bad old days any more, when the natives were fed in like flies! That's no longer economic. From their point of view, of course, many of them work to pay off fiestas or lawyers' fees, rather than have to sell their land; but we need a specialised modern approach. The unions are coming round to it. I've seen great changes."

"So you don't have troubles?"

"Oh no, no troubles at all."

"But I've just read in a local paper that last year there was a massacre—well, not actually in a mine itself, but on land nearby claimed by the company as an extension to one of its cattle ranches, and defended by the occupying Indian community."

"Oh yes? Where did you read that? Of course, the Indians always squabble over boundaries with scant appreciation of the law. The Commies come and whip it up. The police have to deal with them." He chuckled. "It's not England here, you realise. But still, we pretty well keep the peace."

"Though frankly," he added a minute later, his origins wrily breaking the veneer that local family life imposed on him, "I sometimes wish I had never left home."

On which happy note we had beer and sandwiches.

At La Oraya, a junction and mining town laid out with miners' barracks in the shade of a black smelter chimney, a scene that called for a local Lowry, my companion left; and the train swung south down the Mantaro valley, through the ancient settlement of Jauja, whose people for a time had held up the Incas in their north-wards push from Cuzco, so that this town had afterwards become the capital of Chinchay-suyu, the north-west quarter of the Inca world. North and south through here, so my guide book told me (supplemented by a new English translation of the chronicles of Cieza de Léon, the best sixteenth century account of the country) ran the royal Inca road, with a branch to the coast at Pachacamac, just south of Lima: and these interesting historical details I now shared with a new companion, an American armed with three cameras, who all morning had been sniping the view, endlessly consulting his light meter, changing from stills to movie shots, roaming the carriage in case another window offered a better angle to the picture and incidentally to engage in talk. A true American, he liked people. He wanted to tell them who he was. He was now telling me he was an art teacher, recently divorced and on vacation. "I thought I'd see me a bit of the world." We began talking history, art, and photography.

"You going to Huancayo and the Sunday market? They say it's the best thing in the Andes; except for Cuzco," he qualified. He was gratified to hear that I was. Most people in the coach were doing that. It was the regular thing. "My Agency told me." His eye shot over the others to make sure there was no one he had missed.

He glanced outside: and as if an enemy patrol had simultaneously come into view, he twisted up to the top of the window and peppered a wall and an adobe hut.

He decimated the countryside.

This meanwhile was becoming fertile, a riverside scene of rich

fields suitable for growing wheat and barley, and the all-import-
ant Peruvian potato, and quinoa, a kind of millet, and alfalfa:
these fields thinning as they ran up the hillsides to end in scrub
and clumps of thorn and finally the really stony ground. Some
of it was pasture, with black and white cattle; and the sections
divided by screens of eucalyptus and cactus-lined village tracks.
Peasant figures with primitive ploughs were here and there preparing the ground (early October was spring for them), and
close by the train a shepherd boy was throwing stones at straying
sheep; but there were not many such figures in view, a flash of
colour here and there in the dark skirts and mantles of the
women, a straw hat, but otherwise little to personalise them, to
abstract their terracotta faces, their shapes, from the background.
Willingly or not, they were bound up in it.

At stations, however, the peasant throng looked far more
independent. With bundles and baskets, heading for market. The
coffee and chocolate and black of the skirts turned to light blue
for the younger women, with embroidered blouses and rich
mantles, and such a variety of straw hats. Not just this, though, the
ampler look, but the independent vigour of their faces. Cholas?
Mestizas? They had the Indian complexion, but not that earthbound mentality.

Most of them however missed the train. The guard, a mestizo,
waved them back, looking through them as he blew his whistle.

We reached Huancayo in late afternoon, the sky now leaden
and soggy with cloud, the low tile and corrugated roofs glisten-
ing from a recent shower of rain. All those people the American
had talked to went to the central tourist hotel. There was a
scuffle of children in the station yard, a seizing, almost a rape of
suitcases, and pleas even from the ones who missed out for pitiful coins; then though it was only a few minutes walk we were
swept to the door in limousines. Hotel desk. Uniformed porters.
Room with shower overlooking the square. Though difficult to
avoid it was a bit sickening to be gathered again into this routine.

What to do till the next afternoon? There would of course
be the market; though personally, perhaps from the weight of

cliché all such markets carry on their back, I felt a slight resistance there. How to be sure one was even seeing it? It had become, as with all over-advertised products, difficult to get near to. Anyway, that was for next morning.

Now, from the balcony, across the cold square, the rain clouds hesitantly lifting, I could see a few men in ponchos, a stall being dismantled for the night, a country bus lurching in. Lights were going on in shops and workshops, in an administrative and a newspaper office; a political party blared its claims to the presidency in the coming year; lights went on in a restaurant-bar, and along a wall previously in shadow little bundles of men and women, crouching, huddled closely together, were suddenly shown up. At the end of this line two were standing, bare-headed, impassive, mutely staring, as if they were next in turn to be shot. Though these creatures were fifty yards away, so clear was the thin mountain air, even at dusk, that one could study their faces, the lassitude and the non-connection, one could pity their clothes, their horny feet. They floated, enlarged, through the air towards one. It was frightening, disagreeable; but they themselves, at some much deeper level than this, evoked the most disturbing sympathy.

From close to, for I crossed towards them ten minutes later and they hadn't budged, and three hours later when I went to bed they were still precisely in the same place, their countenances were also lined with endless acts of submission and fear. I had never seen such faces in Asia, not even among opium-taking coolies, nor among beggars nor refugees, nor in Africa, nor in any of my travels; but I remembered I had seen such faces on film, when the concentration camps had been opened. Here were the very dregs of suffering.

Well . . . even among dregs, and the slurred pace of their harsh whispers passing down the line sounded like a groping after something lost, there were glances startled into stronger feeling. Was it anger, disdain, the beginnings of mockery? One could only hope so. It was not curiosity.

Next morning began with the sun high, and the market already in full swing, as if magically at the touch of a button. Empty buses, that had disgorged passengers from all the surrounding countryside, were lined beside the railway track. Fresh bread of a dozen varieties gleamed from tall baskets; and a little further on eating stalls were already packed with eaters. In fact, everyone seemed to be eating, in every little corner of activity, putting the day into perspective. It was impossible to resist, and how good it tasted: anticuchos, chicharrones (fried skin of pig in rolls), tamales, soups, and a sort of cornish pasty. I found myself trying the different breads, and washing it all down with tea.

"So," the woman serving me asked, "you are a Señor, a caballero, who is travelling? To see Huancayo?" She grinned. "A gringo?"

Gringo, according to tone of voice, denotes politely or impolitely an outsider, a foreigner with a white skin and Caucasoid features.

I assented.

"And do you like it here?"

"Very civilised," I said. "It seems to be a place of importance. The air is much better than in Lima."

"Ah, Lima, Señor! My son has been there. He was drafted into the army. We tried to stop it, but ay, those brutes, we could not get the right papers. We tried the commandant, the capitán; but I think their army needed my son. He was such a good-looking fellow!" The neighbouring stall women were laughing; she was obviously off on a favourite theme. She was a broad-faced buxom woman, with skin the colour of dark oil, and a straw hat coquettishly above it. "But he is here again now. A licenciado. You can see him marching his men this morning. Ay, ay. I too shall join up, if they take me off to Lima."

Enough listeners had gathered by now, hoping for free entertainment, peeling away from the drift of people circulating between the stalls, and some of their glances were none too friendly and I caught the word gringo and I thought I heard someone suggest that I was a recruiting officer, for me to pay and clear off quickly. Her local Spanish had been difficult to follow, modified, I was to learn later because Emilio's uncle had a similar speech, by Quechua, and by even an earlier Indian dialect. Though seemingly, their Quechua also was corrupted, no longer the broad pliable vehicle of imperial Incaic times; if at all, that was heard only in Cuzco. But so far, it seemed to me, trading was conducted principally in their sort of local Spanish, the prestige tongue; though all around one was the other language with its babbling slightly explosive tempo. "Suma wawa," I had picked up—"oh what a beautiful baby!" So as, when taking photos, to calm suspicions.

Besides the square and other bays of trading the main street, the royal Inca highroad, was given over to it for a full two miles, a ribbon of fruits and grains and tubers, and green coca, and herbs and hides, and baskets and cottons and petticoats, tools and aluminium pots, and hat stall upon hat stall, and more petticoats, and more vegetables: and whilst the central reach of the street was occupied by more expensive goods, and by the sellers of candles and wooden crosses, the further reaches on either side were progressively filled by more modest traders, till one came to the women with a few onions or an old man with a bundle of kindling, entrance tickets so to speak to the great social occasion it was; for they sat by these and there was occasional barter of an onion or two for a few beans, an intercourse of nods and frowns, but as often as not no exchange took place, and certainly no sale. The main thing was to be present.

From a barber's shop I could watch this scene, and be surfeited with creole attention, for the barber and his lads were dandies to a man, talking off-handedly of the capital. What, I asked, would be a good buy here?

The barber shrugged. It depended what I needed. A new wrist watch, a transistor radio? More sensible, of course, to buy them in Lima.

No, local things. Peasant rugs, shawls. Or was there any Indian pottery.

He spat discreetly, as if I had cursed. "Señor, there is nothing I can recommend." And as if to underline his opinion he went to

the door and shooed away a beggar, another of those gaunt sub-
human figures, in tattered poncho and homespun trousers, that
I had seen the night before and once or twice this morning; though
generally today a more robust population, a cheerful, vigorous,
confident peasantry filled the market area. Only static against a
wall, or slumped in a doorway, or on the fringe of the proceedings, loading donkeys or buying a soup, were the unmistakable
bottom layer.

Leaving the barber's, within a stone's throw, I found decorated
gourds and bowls, and a shawl, that a bric-à-brac merchant
would give his eyes for. As well I did, for back at the hotel I
had the Americans to compete with. "Gee, that's smart! Now
look what I got!" To calypsoes we had our rounds of drinks and
were serenaded into lunch.

I didn't expect Brozas till later, in view of the importance of the
midday meal. He was going to introduce me to his uncle before
we caught the overnight bus, but I expected this to be about
teatime. He turned up about three o'clock. In the meantime, over
an uneatable menu served by ponderous peasant waiters (at a
guess, out of the lower levels of the local mestizo ladder), there
had appeared a little company of stiffly dressed starchily mannered
gents with their wives, not a dot or an eyebrow wrong, the very
acme of white culture, modelled, it went without saying, on
Lima, who were perhaps government officials or inspectors, one
was an officer, perhaps another was a merchant or manager of the
agricultural bank, all of the most serious tone, anyway, who had
proceeded to eat the uneatable food with the minimum of gusto.
They came in looking disdainfully indifferent to anything they
were likely to find, bowed unctuously here or there, continued
disdainfully as if all could be endured, and were careful to bow
again as they left. At least, they had kept up with each other.

Brozas was flushed from alcohol, and preoccupied. He extended
a warm sustaining greeting, then fell silent. He was driving a small
Ford truck. We drove the few yards to the bus depot, checked our
seats, I paid what I owed, then we stood at the edge of the square,
pondering. He was wearing a check shirt, jeans, and an old

corduroy jacket. He still looked, however, an intellectual, a seeker and a teacher.

I asked him about the derelict Indians, once again crouching along the wall, as the market began to be dismantled.

He was not quite with me, his tone was mechanical—"They wear typical clothing, especially the women, that they make in their own communities. The babies are swaddled and carried on the back. They live in extended family groups and divide the work traditionally. They are illiterate, speak Quechua, rarely Spanish. All the men chew coca. Yes..." He paused. "Yes, it's like that. There's much besides. Their music, fiestas, certain foods, the systems of communal help called minka, then the ayni, and their tributary labour; and then other practices like trial marriage—well, you ask me a lot, I think. But it's true to say that even in the most remote community there are elements of European culture, in their tools, ideas, in many things. Nothing is purely Indian any more; there's always a fraction of outside influence. There have been developments in each century."

"But are those community Indians?"

"No, round here the communities are better off, relatively speaking; you'll find a difference in the south of Peru. Those could be landless Indians, working for a few soles a day for a hacienda, and for some of their keep, but certain to be heavily in debt; or more likely they do odd jobs in town. They do look at their last gasp—it's an accumulation of grievance and despair. Don't listen too much to talk about coca. That is only one element. We'll try some later."

"Oh, I see." But seeing very little, I tried to prise more details out of him—"they're not cholos?"

"Oh no, no. Cholos are the more energetic Indians, they may work the land themselves or for a master, or do crafts or trade, but they think differently—they're modern, independent, material-istic. They've moved out of the larger-unit life. They run this sort of market. There's no limit to their ambitions. They are really the most interesting class in Peru, and a lot of mestizos are 'cholified' too. It's correctly a question of how they think of themselves."

"Not necessarily to do with race, or colour?"

"Well, these terms . . ." He smiled, becoming drawn in. "Different people will tell you different things, and there are differences in every province of the country. But roughly, it is as I am telling you. My family, for instance, are town mestizos. We lived in Huancayo as far back as we remember, and we've traded with Lima since 1900. Now, an Indian who worked for us as a peon got on, he moved into a village of cholo weavers, he adapted, advanced, and today he's in Lima, a much richer trader than my uncle. When he comes back here, they call him 'Don'; to Indian eyes he's 'white', a rich man; but he thinks of himself always as cholo. He's really a sort of super-cholo. The economic man of the present."

"Will such people take over Peru?"

"Oh, eventually, without question."

"Let us go," he said. "My family awaits us." He was more lively now, and he took my arm as if I had done him a small service.

Brozas was Emilio Espiritu Brozas, with his mother's name, Salazar; and his uncle was Paul Fortunate Brozas, with a mother's family of Guzman; and they were, to judge by their town house, which was unpretentious and decaying but spaciously arranged around a garden patio, and near to the square, an old-established middle class family of the province, as he himself had said. Emilio (I now thought of him as Emilio, and soon called him such) had looked dark-skinned down in Lima; but up here, among the terracotta and chocolate, he and his uncle and all their group looked of relatively light complexion, more or less a nicely-burnished copper. They were all very jolly when we appeared, though with certain inbred restraints, a desire to keep a certain refinement, a certain availability for serious discussion, however much drink they consumed. They were a group of decent church people.

Emilio related my interest in the Indians, and his uncle, making sure I had a glass of the home-brewed chicha they were drinking, and taking a good sip at his own, took up the topic—"most honoured señor, I am an employer of many Indians. I am their father, and they are my children. Some of them lie, some of them steal, they can be lazy, and they carry disease, but . . . deep down, they are good people! They also have Christian souls, Señor. They have diligence, fidelity. I am proud to have their blood in my veins" . . . there were one or two happy nods from his audience, otherwise slightly fuddled attention . . . "I have good relations with my Indians, my friend. They come to me. I am their compadre. I protect them before the law. Where would they be without that?"

Emilio was displaying a smiling politeness, but his brow was starting to furrow again. I was beginning to construct his story in my mind: his radicalism, his grip on the students, the corner he had built for himself in Lima, set against this minor patriarchal background. But where were his own parents; and how much did he owe to Juanita? Why were they living so humbly? Unostentatiously, it was well-to-do-here.

His uncle was continuing, "I understand suffering, for, for thirty years we have been persecuted. I and all my family, Señor, because of our political beliefs. With APRA we have stood for the Indians, for justice and progress, and against imperialism. We reject the concessions made by Leguia! We reject the presence of Yankee exploiters! And every prefect and police commandant in Huancayo has borne down upon us. We, good men of Huancayo, made to suffer by men from Lima!"

"Yes, yes, Compa Páu," said another oldish man, soothingly, grinning in his cups, "till now, Compa Páu. Now you hold office. They'll have to make you the next mayor."

"That could be, Pa Mígue, if God so wills it. Our movement has destiny behind it. Look how we dealt with Odria in winter, when he dared to show his face again here! The once great dictator, pelted with stones." He began smiling to himself with grumbling amusement.

Emilio frowned harder. "But, uncle . . ." Then he shrugged.

He was restless, no longer joining in the drinking. "But, uncle, you of APRA have sold your souls. It's Beltran, Prado, not destiny behind you."

His uncle coloured, to a very deep copper, then smiled a bit roguishly. "It is we, more truthfully, behind them, Emilio! In order, as you know, to regain a foothold; to be allowed at last, from 1956, to speak and work before the law." He turned again to me, "Please tell your countrymen, most worthy Señor, and my friend, that APRA now casts off this alliance! We fight again as an independent force. We proceed with the revolution."

Emilio scowled. "What revolution, uncle? What would you do, in truth, if . . . ?" Then he shrugged again, and one of the women intervened, in an atmosphere that quivered suddenly, with insistence on our eating another meal, with that long night journey ahead.

So the uncle only said, "My child, please, never forget the years of suffering, and of exile, and of brutal death. Whoever carries on, we paved the way."

"No, uncle, I do not forget." And Emilio looked more than just politely grave.

Then the chicha was served round again, and with many Saluds all drank and rejoiced in the conviviality of the Sabbath. Emilio again made his contribution; he told them stories to make them laugh; he had changed easily, yet somewhere he was frowning still, and questing and pondering.

A table was laid in the next room, and not just we, the two travellers, sat down to it, but the entire family group again. "Compa Páu, your very good health!"

The women served us. It was succulent lamb. "Pa Mígue, when they elect me mayor, I shall give a fiesta such as you have never seen!"

"Salud!" "Salud!" I started to wonder how much chicha I could take.

"No harm in getting drunk," observed Emilio; "it always makes the journey shorter."

"Only madmen take that bus. And now the rains have started

too." And eagerly, between rejoicing as farmers for the advent of the long-awaited rain, they plunged into horror stories. Deaths, catastrophes on that road, the worst road, they assured me, in all Peru.

"They're only teasing you," said Emilio.

Shortly after this we got ready.

The bus was late in getting away. Some passengers had taken their seats, stuffing the rack above them with parcels, others had got down again to re-enter the office and argue with the agent or complain at the boy on the bus roof stowing away their luggage, or to walk up and down and grumble to the friends who had come to see them off. It had been raining again, dusk was menacing with streaks of orange in a gunmetal sky: everyone was talking about it and how the road would be washed away, and that it was folly to travel at all.

Then order descended. The tarpaulin was in place. The agent, a vast oak of a man with an explosively thick nut-brown visage, appeared on the pavement, and the bus filled. A teenage conductor and a driver who was shorter and frailer than the wheel he had to handle took over, and with a skid we had shot away. There was a last glimpse of the Sunday piazza and the people sensibly staying at home.

The conductor checked us by his list and shifted one or two passengers. At the front were a young wide-awake couple with highly artificial manners, air travel bags, and a basic joke that contented them till they fell asleep; behind them a lawyer and a fat civilian who was entered on the list as a captain, who was at once in trouble because of some boxes a friend had brought him at the last moment that now protruded from under the seat. But he was too drunk to do anything about them, and testily the conductor moved on. Across the gangway was a doctor, a merchant, a woman in mourning accompanied by a nun; then Emilio and myself, then a young cadet who progressively slackened the look of his uniform, then grandmother, mother, and infant baby, the baby in a fastidious pink layette that was repeatedly changed through the stations of the night, in between cries and suckling noises; then various men. And then began, in an atmosphere noticeably denser for traces of it floated forward, the second more rustic half of the company, men, women, and children wrapped to the eyes, staring fixedly as if they could see, and possibly hear ahead of the driver, silent except to spit occasionally—the darker half that this bus like the nation had to accept as belonging to it. On the back bench were five young Indians, moodily drunk, who ignored the conductor when he ordered them to move some sacks. He returned forward in a vile temper.

The radio was playing and the front passengers were all conversing, so it was easy for Emilio to say things that he might not want others to hear. He was retracing his uncle's point of view. An absolutely fair man, he was admitting APRA's pioneering role, and saying yes, the degree of organisation now found among the unions, in the mines, in transport, and on the coast plantations, had primarily APRA to thank. Huancayo, undoubtedly, was progressive in education: much of that due to APRA. When we returned to Lima he would take me to the magnificent party centre, with its clinics and classes in welfare and art. All that, and more.

"APRA means Alianza Popular Revolucionaria Americana. But," he scoffed, "it has joined a very dubious alliance; it has forfeited much of its popularity; it would be truer to call it counter-revolutionary; and as for the last word, if Haya had been logical, he would have made it Indo-Americana! Haya de la Torre, in 1923, when he led the students against Leguia—for my uncle, you saw, that's still an issue—was the hope of the left wing. He was a disciple of Mariategui. After that, well, he wasn't always at the head of his followers when he should have been. Some personal weakness there. But in the main, the stage was insufficiently prepared, and the oligarchy that runs Peru contained the movement. Some were exiled, some shot. Many were imprisoned. The twenties and the thirties were terrible for APRA. They won an election in 1936, as they did again in 1945:

but both times the army stepped in. As already they are hinting they'll do again if APRA comes to the top next year."

"I thought APRA was in the present government?"

"Yes, that's it. They've fitted in. Registered under a different name. They've used their votes to take orders and jobs from the landowners and the bankers. So are they any more their opponents? Hasn't exile and imprisonment taught its lesson? APRA leaders are now past middle age, after a lifetime in opposition. I doubt they'll risk any more of that."

"You see," he added, "for being Apristas, my grandfather was shot in the thirties; and twelve years ago my father disappeared, arrested one night in Lima. My mother died a year later. APRA has too much taken the brunt. I doubt it has got any guts left in it. That's why I'm forced to a more radical party."

"But you just said the generals are afraid of APRA getting to power on its own ticket?"

"Yes, yes; there are many personal feuds. That's all criollo politics. And then, it has a Fidelista wing—not that my uncle and his kind encourage it!"

Emilio was thoroughly himself again, crisp and humorous and scathingly thoughtful, not prepared to dodge any point. We were smoking; it neutralised the smells, though the smells were welcome as part of the blanket the bus was building up against the cold night air. The driver was a maniac. We rocked and bounced as we slewed past other traffic. The headlights suddenly revealed some peasants, like rabbits round a turn in the road, rooted helplessly to the spot they were on. Three men were holding one another up. A woman was squatting, urinating. Another woman was reslinging her baby. As we fell upon them the men collapsed, the women screamed and tugged at the men; but we had shot to the side, inclined steeply, and ricocheted away.

"You see," said Emilio, "this afternoon I had already been disputing with my uncle. For the truth is, as he now holds office, he took no part against Odria a few months back; he only claims it when he drinks. He has lost his power of action. And this very day, news is coming through about a rising of several thousand peasants of the Yarusyacán Indian community. It seems they have invaded Hacienda Paria, that belongs to the Cerro de Pasco company, the American mining corporation, re-occupying land they claim is theirs. You know, this is one of the most critical issues. It's been going on for decades, centuries, in every corner of our country. The Indian communities being squeezed out; and without knowing the legal facts in this case, it's just one more terrible instance of an overall wrong set of possibilities. It just should never arise. And last year this same hacienda had a fight on its hands with the Rancas community."

"I've read about that. I was talking to one—"

"Yes," said Emilio, pressing his conclusion, "you see, don't you, it should never arise? And the troops and police should not be used to support the rich and butcher the poor? As today they've already been called on again. Yet my uncle will not see this now. He talks of legal documents. But how much does a judge cost here, or a lawyer, or a string of witnesses? What do they pay for a chief of police or a full-blown general? The country has got to have a revolution! How else will anything change!"

"That's my dilemma," he added quietly, a moment later as his fury cooled, "for I can't work with the Communists. I don't like Communism."

He was silent, as was the whole bus now, not through listening in to him, but because the first conversations had ended, we had halted twice to deliver packages, slithering whirring forward again to the growing downbeat of the rain; lightning had flashed in the hills ahead; the road was rougher, the view nothing but rocks and verges we just avoided. The real night journey had begun. What an inane thing to be doing! Perhaps everyone thought this; they were attempting sleep. Except for the frail microscopic driver, and the conductor and another chum, who like a team of three on a rope seemed just to get us round those corners, their faces craning towards the windscreen.

Lights came at us round a bend, we dipped ours and drew to the side; at the next bend we dipped and flashed, and came on a convoy of waiting trucks like grey moths against the cliff. We swung past, then immediately braked, to inch through a torrent across the road that could be heard like a waterfall below us. Trees gleamed and blew with the rain; but it was comforting to see trees, and muddy fields swinging up beside us, and to feel some rock shaking one's bones, rather than to imagine precipices and road cuts through crumbling earth. We nosed our way over bridges no wider than we, the swirling waters caught for an instant in the headlights; we shot past farms and through villages that already in part looked flooded and abandoned; then the rain swept at us with redoubled force as the valley narrowed and we began descending—or was it ascending, in the dark and the rain it was no longer possible to distinguish—and the view lost all definition, and we began to slither; and we had come to a stop.

"Fifteen minutes," barked the conductor, as he and the driver jumped out. One could see now the lights of an inn, and the outlines of other buildings. "Good," said Emilio, coming to life, "let's refresh ourselves."

Ten minutes later the rain had abated, and there was no more than a drizzle as we stood by the door, a quantity of pisco inside us. In the warm interior passengers were still gobbling plates of stew, a tall hawk-faced proprietress scurrying the serving wenches round; outside, in the murk, the driver checked a wheel and hailed a lorry that pulled in, and beyond him, facing this way or that, indifferent to what they were doing, both men and women from the peasants we were carrying pulled open their pants or squatted to urinate, and beyond them, huddled in a doorway, a row of silent shadowy men, villagers or apparitions, stared through us to the back of beyond. "It's a tricky road from this point on." Emilio twinkled. "Our pass with fate."

We were off. Renewed conversation. An argument started up behind us between one of the drunk Indian youths, who had moved up the gangway, sitting on a sack, and a grey-faced man in a collar and tie. "I'm an obrero, a workman," the youth was saying in very soft mestizo Spanish, "I don't take orders from you. I've learned my work; it's that which counts. I don't look up to you any longer." One couldn't hear what the other said, though he looked sick to the gills with disgust; the youth was out to make a scene. "I've worked as far north as Chimbote. I've earned money, not patrons' favours. You must say Señor when you speak to me."

The whole bus was now listening and the conductor thrusting along the gangway.

"To your seat!" he cried. "Keep the gangway clear."

The youth glared sullenly at him. "I am speaking to this caballero," he began—

"Go back or I'll turn you off the bus."

The Indian glowered. "I hold a ticket. Is it necessary that I show it to you?" There was a small glint of amusement some-where in the dark ochre of his features. He was sneering.

The conductor, waving his arms like fists, repeated his threats, but made no impression. But the rise of protest from other passengers, a chorus of oblique indignation, seeming actually to surprise the youth, unseated him. He scowled and retired.

The indignation became more voluble, once the threat of violence had passed. Several passengers stopped the conductor and argued their solidarity with him. An insult to all decent people! Those animals shouldn't be allowed on buses. One little whisp of a man, as dark in texture as the offending youth and wearing a crushed shabby suit, proclaimed that the police should be informed. There were nods. The air bristled with hostility. Then as quickly the incident faded out.

Meanwhile the bus had been picking its way with a good deal more caution. At first it seemed as if we were climbing, but the cliff above and the cliff beneath and the debris which we were skirting round, and the constant though muffled roar of the river, suddenly suggested we were edging along the side of a rather ominous gorge. Water spouted on to the road in fast thick falls. There was mist. The verge, beyond which the drop commenced, did not look too solid. Then out of the mist came a loaded truck and both vehicles halted.

The conductor and the driver got out, examined the ground,

then went to do a pee. The driver of the truck stayed where he was. It had stopped raining, and the captain in the seat ahead said we should all have to get out of the bus. He must have gathered I was an Englishman, for, "Do you have roads like this in England?"

"We don't have mountains like this in England."

"Every year this road collapses." He spoke with grave drunken equanimity. "Trucks and buses drop into the river. It is a disgrace, Señor. We are a poor people."

"You are very rich in rain, anyway."

He liked that and a few minutes later was repeating it to the sleepy lawyer.

He came back, "Please ask me anything you wish. It is an honour to be of service, Señor. We can talk. There is all night ahead of us. Are you proceeding to Ayacucho?"

"Yes, to Huamanga University."

"What an honour!" But then he lost interest.

The bus crawled up to the truck and put its bonnet alongside. The truck was up to the cliff wall so presumably felt it could do no more. If the road held we could get by. Everyone craned to the windows, through which next to nothing could be seen, and the conductor leaned out of the doorway. We edged ahead, then stopped again. The conductor had decided that too much water was pouring across the patch ahead, and that it would be fatal to continue. As if all his accumulated spleen saw a legitimate opening, he leaped down, ran round to the truck, and abused its driver with instructions.

After a time, and a few retorts, the other complied and began to reverse. We followed, and to our horror saw the truck almost go over the edge as swirls of Scotch mist enveloped it, but then discovered that that was the road doubling on itself at that point; then we were past, and as if in celebration or perhaps irritated by his conductor the driver put on a show of speed. Perilously, we skidded ahead. Down, down, in a cauldron of mist—but was this the sensation of dropping?—and then abruptly we were on a rocky surface and across a bridge and out of the gorge. The air before us suddenly cleared. Just past midnight, somewhere in the Andes.

Huanta, a market town. From here to Ayacucho, a negligible run with paltry climbs; one could safely sleep. So it had not been much of an adventure, after all.

But that was to be over-sanguine. I remember waking from a dream in which my head was splitting open, to find myself thrown against the seat in front, shocked by pain growing out of numbness, ears ringing then exploding with a chorus of shattering glass, screams and thuds, and the memory of the crash itself. I couldn't extricate my feet. There they were. In a second I had joined everyone else trying to get out of the bus. Emilio followed and had the presence of mind to bring out two small cases with him. My first impression was one of relief: no precipices, only gulleys, into one of which the bus had turned, a front-wheel skid that had hit a rock. A wing was smashed, the bonnet was steaming; the remaining headlight lit up a road and craggy hill panorama entirely covered with snow. It was bitter. It was the summit of the earth and the wind went through one. Emilio had already turned down the road, tugging at me, and I was shambling after. The Indians, shadowy, were doing the same. Another vehicle was coming up behind. The middle class mestizo gentry were still crowding about the bus, beginning to upbraid the driver. We put on speed as Emilio called, "No time to waste. I know." I began to feel hilariously well.

We reached what was a truck, a sort of covered waggon, after the Indians, who had stopped it; but as yet they had not been allowed to climb on. The driver turned to listen to Emilio. Emilio spoke to him in Quechua, a seemingly endless exchange; but with a final "Si, si, patron", we were motioned inside—not into the cab, but into the wigwam part that was already filled with huddled bodies, sacks, a piece of machinery, and a pig. The smell, though not from the pig, was awful. Two Indians came in on top of us, the rest being left by the way. The truck juddered along to the bus. "Now," said Emilio, slyly, wryly, as he continued to rub himself all over, "you listen! The gentry will have to pay."

There was a frantic scene, no quarter given: the upshot being that the fat captain and the grandmother, mother, and infant were taken into the cab at the highest price, half a dozen others at the next price were introduced into the back in place of peasants there who were ejected, and then those peasants, the original occupants, plus the people who had been in the cab, plus our Indians who had grown to about six, together with one or two bits of luggage, were allowed or not allowed, it didn't matter, as the truck had again started away, the driver in a temper, in on top of us. This was impossible, so some of them clung somehow to the framework. The night was blacked out by bodies. One could hear shouts from the bus lessening—though of course other trucks would be along. The question was, could this one make it? It juddered and groaned up an endless incline, but fortunately, at the critical moment, always seemed to have a lower gear.

Emilio and the others returned to sleep. I couldn't. It was the smell of coca. The pig and the rest of it I was perfectly used to from journeys round and about Greece; but the coca absolutely nailed me. I watched an Indian, silhouetted in the sickly dawn breaking upon us, shift the bolus about in his mouth from one cheek to the other. Seemingly, in the two hours of the run, he would have been extracting about eighty per cent of the chew, ten grams of coca leaf and lime yielding eight centigrams of cocaine. Very nice for him.

Pas pour moi.

It was just a week since I had entered Peru and once again I was sitting in a café. But now it was in the alpine air, the eternally spring air they claimed, of Ayacucho in the central Andes, in a valley of orchards at nine thousand feet, capital of a Department that stretched from the jungle along the river Apurimac, a main tributary of the Amazon, over the cordillera to the coast. This in its high mountain fastness was an ancient centre, it was supposed now of the Tiahuanaco culture that had slightly predated the

Incas; it had been the midway post between Lima and Cuzco
for the Conquistadors; and here in 1824 Sucre and his attendant
marshals had battled and decisively won continental independence
from Spain. His statue stood in the middle of the square, a horseback general waving a sword, a stone's throw from where we
were sitting.

I was playing chess with a young American who was attached
to the University. Our pavement table was in the sun, silently
watched by a group of urchins who had drifted over from a blind
fiddler. His music scratched the crisp air, the fortunately hygienic
air I was thinking as I looked at them and at him and at the men
slumped on the benches surrounding Sucre, and at the even more
collapsed figures against the fine old colonnades. Ayacucho was
billed in my guide book as a corner of sixteenth century Spain;
and in the plenitude of gilded churches, town houses with large
patios, shaded terraces, carved stonework, squarely set about the
square, this was true if one overlooked their condition; otherwise, in the human material, the neat white-shirted schoolgirls
as much as the besotted peasants, the confident mechanics and
chola women as much as the police or half-starved students, this
was contemporary Latin America. It was like Huancayo, only
smaller, poorer. Straw hats had become felt hats. Desperation a
twist more desperate. Even the landlords were less well off.

There were rather a lot of priests about, suggesting some
church election. I noticed also how the peasant women while
walking, as I remembered it in Greece, spun coarse yarn on
spindles they kept twisting with their right hand. There was also
a constant passage of men burdened sometimes as high again by
bales or boxes roped to their back, their faces down towards their
bare feet, going by at a smart shuffle. And there was a boy
circulating with the Lima papers, two days old.

"Your move."

Q-B5; then as before a few minutes in which to let one's
attention wander.

The most amazing piece of luck here, though, had been running
into Azuarga. Besides being a prominent novelist, he was a tele-

vision contributor, as earlier he had worked for radio and a
paper; and he was here considering the possibilities along with
some Americans of a short film, either, as he said in his fierce
way of inviting everyone else's opinion, on the current revival of
the town's life around Huamanga University or on the work of
Don Joaquin Lopez. Don Joaquin was a folk sculptor of crucifixes
and saints and thumb-sized altar pieces; he was an extraordinary
artist.

We were all dining with the professors. The University had
been founded in 1677, but after the town's marked decline had
been closed in 1886; to be reopened two years ago under the
guidance of a courageous man, the Rector, Dr Fernando Romero.
For six years it could be largely non-political: the emphasis could
be on study. This was the challenge: to show Peru that a serious
regionally-orientated centre of mainly higher technical studies
could be made to work. A quarter of the students were drawn
from the coast, all had to learn Quechua; their subjects were
firstly education, agricultural engineering, anthropology, mining,
and industrial chemistry, then biology and social service; and
there were field activities, in farming, health, and education, in a
depressed pampa area nearby where they could practise what
they were learning. Seventy per cent of these students, however,
half-starved in the very meanest lodgings, and they had to do
their studies by daytime or else standing about in this square
reading under the weak electric lamps. Ayacucho lacked electricity; the University overall funds. Hence, with all the ambivalence
it gave rise to, the need to interest Americans.

The professors were a wonderful crowd, of both sexes, like the
students. An innovation for Peru, they were employed full-
time; a few of them were of other nationalities; and all were
contributing out of their salaries to aid urgent student needs.
They were a great team, idealists, experimenters, who had had to
contend with local animosity from priests and lawyers who had
seen the college as an opportunity for more personal perks; their
work thrust out into schools, kindergartens, the hospital, and
adult education. For the first time under such auspices, masons

and merchants, chauffeurs and musicians, tailors, policemen, bakers, housewives, were sitting together to learn English, or mathematics, family welfare, or the writing of Spanish. New life had come to Ayacucho. Economically there was a new rhythm, with fewer people going to the coast. Public administration had improved. No wonder Azuarga felt he had a theme.

He was a short, broad-shouldered man, a doctor's son from Cuzco. He enjoyed disparaging Lima and Limeñans, an unnecessary foreign fungus, he called it. "The capital should be at Pucallpa! Or, yes—there's Cuzco!" He had a fierce wry style of conversation. A joke was often an underhand thrust. He was rather ugly, with the inevitable moustache. Not in the least restless or unsure, he just pushed work ahead with speed and acumen. He listened to everybody's ideas, then, the next thing, he had started something. But at that point he never explained. He kept crossing the square, urging on some companion; he was absorbing, analysing, remaking the town.

My move again; and now Azuarga together with Emilio appeared on the porch of the University. They stopped to read a large notice: a lecture with slides on Gauguin for the evening. They had only met at lunch today among the high-spirited professorial chatter. Perhaps the indecision in Emilio, the continuing quest that finely informed his serious and intelligent nature, was irresistible for the more ruthless man. Not that Azuarga had the answers, but given this opening he would start constructing them.

They came over. It was fixed. The three of us together were going out to the pampa tomorrow. Emilio would be staying there some weeks, for his survey and to help with training, Azuarga and I for a night or so. I already had a plane seat booked for Lima in four days' time.

My opponent at this point claimed the game. A quiet, a very quiet, American.

Next morning early we hit the trail, a real nerve thumper of a road, over bleak moorland; we smoked and talked; to arrive at last in a thin little village with a general store, two stores selling

coca, and a few thatch or red-tiled dwellings built up with stone
and adobe. Other dwellings stretched across the pampa near to
their owners' fields. A tractor stood thick with mud. A mule
pack laden with pelts was departing up a long valley, dotted with
sheep, the old shepherd and his wife sitting near where the road
looped down, both of them hand-spinning wool. A lad with an
oil drum roped to him was delivering water to the houses. There
was a school building a few miles off, near the agricultural centre,
and another village of Marochuko farmers, a curious blond blue-
eyed pocket whose ancestors were said to have been deserters
from one of the conquering Spanish forces. All the people in
view, and those later, without saying were poor, but tough and
independent. Till now an average of twenty-five thousand per
year had been leaving the Department for the coast; the
University, by showing new techniques, and by arranging loans,
hoped to stop some of them. Emilio was soon into the thick of it.

I mooched about with Azuarga. A countryman himself, this
scene was familiar. I was not surprised to learn that his father, the
doctor, had also owned a small property and that his childhood
had been spent in woods and fields: this came out in his writing.
What had turned him into a rebel? Not his father; the doctor had
spent a lifetime protecting Indians. Not even Cuzco feudalism—
no, firstly, it had been his need to write simple and honest Spanish;
struggling with words he had found himself struggling with
everything in that environment. You couldn't put together an
honest sentence if you accepted a morally squalid society. Thus
hour by hour he had cleansed his views. And with each book they
became fiercer! "It's the logic of grammar. My dialectic." His
face contorted as he threw this out. He hunched his shoulders,
swung them free.

We were watching the trade in coca, and Azuarga joined in the
peasants' talk. His Quechua was like a fusillade. He seemingly
punctured them with his thoughts, for a drawn-out silence followed. "Fools," he commented, in his soft harsh castellano,
"they were afraid you might bewitch their women with your
strange white face. They are convinced you must have magical

powers." He went for them again; then, pleased with himself, cried, "Come. Follow. There's a sick child. I've said that you are willing to help."

"But—"

"Come. We look inside the house. Everything is set for the curandero. It's fascinating, isn't it, for you?"

Unscrupulously, pushing her ahead, he marshalled one of the women's steps. We went round to a particularly mean dwelling, an outhouse at the back of a wall, with a low square door and no windows. Inside there was barely room for us. On a raised earth platform at one end lay a girl child wrapped in cloths, listlessly distraught and sweating. Away from her, lit, near the wall, by candles, were some objects the centrepiece of which was a mounted wooden crucifix painted blue and red and white with the face of Christ sculptured on to it. The mother knelt and crossed herself, then began yapping at Azuarga. In the shadows behind us were a few bits of clothing hung up on nails, some cooking pots, and a thumb-sized store half-filled with sacks. Nothing else. Stone and mud walls.

Azuarga hushed her pleading, and pointed to the collection of objects. Herbs, fruit, some wizened flower petals collected at a church procession, what looked like a patent powder, cigarettes, coca leaf, and the crucifix. "There you have the history of the Andes over a thousand years," he commented; "and the main item there is the coca. Never underestimate the coca. Without it these people could not exist."

"Brozas tends to play it down."

"That shows there are two points of view, then, doesn't it?" He smiled fiercely. He looked at the patient. "This child ought to see a doctor. It could be a chill, it could be pneumonia. The mother, on the contrary, believes it's the Devil, who entered while the body was frightened, in turn caused by an unclean stomach. She is waiting for the curandero, who locally is also the midwife; but that personage is out of the district. I think you had better prescribe aspirin." He turned to the mother. "I'll tell her for you. Then you speak something in English."

Instead I took the poor child's arm, stiff and a bit swollen, and stroked it for a moment. Her dark sheep eyes. Her dirty skin. This manger.

Poor helpless child, born here.

Reason enough to turn anyone rebel.

We ate in a larger version of the same kind of dwelling. At the end was a half-partitioned kitchen, with meat and a bird hung up against the fly-crawling adobe. A goat was tethered, there were chickens, a dog. There were weighing scales and sweets for sale, and all around us a display of calendars, an orgy of pink pin-up girls. Children, their hair caked with dirt, trailed and swung about the door, the little girls dressed like their mother even to the old felt hat. That worthy was cooking and laying the table with dirty cutlery and even dirtier glasses. Emilio and Azuarga and a resident anthropologist wiped their knives and forks on some paper, but didn't shrink from using the glasses. When the meal came it consisted of a very hot consommé, then trout with rice and a raw onion. Then coffee. The others washed this down with beer.

Then they discussed the rest of the day.

I think Azuarga had had enough. He said, "What do you think one could use particularly from this area? Yes, I too. The working of the school?" Emilio, typically, was pushing the school. "Yes; yes, yes. And even the tractor? I see. Certainly. And are there any of Don Joaquin's altar pieces here?" He quizzed the anthropologist. "I've seen a crucifix; but are there also any retablos? No? I'm sure there must be one. Perhaps we should go on to Cangallo?"

That was awkward, so they continued discussing other things he might care to see. He was fiendishly indulgent, but it gradually emerged that all he wanted was to return to Ayacucho. Whatever enthusiasm had brought him out here, some flame-shot thought in the Rector's office, it had died. And he meant to have his way.

So we spent the afternoon in the fields, looking at potatoes and discussing blight, then exclaiming over some prize pigs; then he and I returned to town, getting a lift in a government truck.

Even more than he by then I was for it. Ayacucho called like a great metropolis.

Still, Azuarga felt, or decided to feel, that he had lured me from some duty or pleasure—the countryside after all, each primitive plough, or women singing as they planted quinoa, was biblical and a sight to see; and he insisted that he owed compensation. Next morning hurrying across the square, he stopped, came over, and proposed I should accompany him on a visit to Don Joaquin. Also, talking ten to the dozen, analysing and constructing, he realised he had found a pupil.

The houses down the street were joined in a white plastered wall, single-storey, red-tiled, with barred windows and narrow doors. Most doors led to the main or the single room of the household, beyond which one could see a yard; but at Don Joaquin's one first entered the yard, flower-filled, hung with laundry, and here in one corner, with his house alongside and other stores across the cobbles, sat the master artisan. He was proud to think of himself as mestizo and of what he was making as mestizo art, a compound of Spanish culture and religion and the popular life and myths of the province. He wore a dark felt hat, sat in shirt sleeves, his fingers moulding the ball of paste, a mixture of gypsum and ground potato, from which he would carve the tiny figures of saints, peasants, and animals for the interior of his altar pieces. These, opening like a triptych, were foot high boxes, painted outside and in, and with the doors turned back one looked at a stage, two-tier, filled with the figures which now were glazed and brightly painted and set to represent two scenes.

The one I bought from him, which was typical, upstairs showed a company of saints, patrons of the animals (especially San Marcos, patron of the bull, who gave his name to the work as a whole) together with various animals and birds; while downstairs was a multiple scene which showed in part a country gathering of peasants and musicians and more animals in front of a table spread with food, but principally was concerned with other figures placed at the back behind the table. These were firstly a rich landlord, his kneeling sons, imploring women, then a miserable shepherd tied to a tree and an overseer with a raised whip. The shepherd was accused of stealing a sheep and so was duly about to be flogged—in fact, the classic colonial scene, the reaffirmation of brute force, the showing of the whip which is an inevitable complement to the other proud habit of showing the flag, with its degradation all round, and suffering. Don Joaquin called this "Las Pasiones".

"Odd," I said to Azuarga, "but my first afternoon in Peru I read in a paper of a similar incident. I mean, now, last year, near Cuzco."

"I know. I grew up among it."

"I wondered if it were just propaganda? I mean, long ago, obviously."

He laughed savagely. "You go and tell the world about it and the bastards will try to cut your throat! Or muzzle you in some way or another. The unpalatable truth! That's where it hurts." He paused. "Why don't you, anyway, if you write? As you're getting close to the bone in our country, you can't stay uncommitted."

"It's hardly my affair—"

"It's Russia's affair. In their own opinion it's China's affair. So better be quick you Anglo-Saxons, and far-off comfortably off Europeans, and think again. Take a look, quick, at Latin America! Right. Answer me: which half of the world will its millions belong to in fifteen years' time, eh? Ah." He twisted about. "Or carry on, if you choose," he scoffed, "as a harmless camera-carrying tourist!"

I had just paid for my San Marcos and been allowed to photograph the artist.

Silently we returned up the street.

"Forgive me," he continued in a conciliatory voice, "but you're a stranger, a writer—who else can one be frank with? What happens if we get another dictatorship? Don't be so sure that that's ruled out. People like you have to tell the truth in case we inside are stopped. As we were, effectively, up to five years ago. Are you a Communist?"

"No, I am not."

"Good, you're in the clear. Start taking notes."

Then abruptly he changed the subject.

In the evening he caught hold of me again. "I'm coming for you early in the morning," he cried; "I owe you a gift after that lecture! It'll be a daylong party. A family affair, but they're letting us in as a favour to their compadre, Don Joaquin. You and myself and Mr Wilson." Wilson was an American cameraman. "Bring plenty of coins with you. Do you know what a compadre is?"

"The godfather of one's child, isn't he? The co-father. Or comadre, the co-mother. Compadrazgo, the network that forms. They have it in Spain, obviously; and in Greece. A very close relationship."

"Basic! Closer than your British Old Boy network! But we also use it lightly, among friends. In that sense, you are my compadre."

And he twisted away, fierce, strange.

Next morning at eight we went to the fiesta, in the large yard of a house, or it might have been an inn, in the Santa Anna quarter of the town. The family had once been muleteers, their womenfolk weavers, and they had carried Don Joaquin's products to all corners of the province, to valleys where a priest rarely went, where prayers and magic were set up around these folktale altars. This trade was dying. The muleteers were combining to run a truck.

We were late. From seven in the morning the chicha had been going round. The yard already reeled with guests, sober-suited, the women flaunting their long wide petticoats and gypsy-rich blouses. There was a drummer, a flautist, and guitar players; Ayacucho was a centre for guitars. The music was the highland huayno. In the porch at one side sat the father with his chief male relatives, his compadres, his brother officers of the local church, and one or two other dignitaries, all suitably glazed with drink. Evidently, two fiestas were being combined: one to celebrate the completion of repairs by the community group to their local church, the other a purely family affair for a child a year old whose hair must be cut, with various other implications: and moreover the fun had already been on for the last twenty-four hours. They had slept in between, but not enough to sober up; and after my third glass of chicha, scooped up from a bucket, I understood. It was going to be a heavy session.

Off gourd dishes and some plates we ate potato and a hot meat hash, and a potato soup, and a maize pudding: that helped a little, for the chicha relentlessly, and doses of alcohol and water, were served round and one could not refuse. There was an element of challenge in this drinking. Very careful watching to see if you cheated, then "Salud!" and laughter, and belches of approval. The music whined away in the background. The dancing sometimes filled the centre space, then thinned away completely. A woman was sobbing, the tears mixing with the chicha that dribbled out of her mouth. From a side room came sounds of an argument, and after a time two men ran out, hitting but mainly menacing each other. They were at once restrained, whereupon they went wild, others joined in and it looked as if a general fight might develop. But a man like a master of ceremonies intervened, his paler face perhaps doing the trick, and the commotion dissolved and the drinking continued. The drinking became more serious now. The musicians were equally into their cups. People between laughter and runs of talk were getting very tearful indeed. It was a real old bum session. The dancers were all over the place. A man was sick, spewing on the floor; a drunken woman mopped it up; everyone else found it hilarious. Round and round the chicha went. It was a real old nursery session.

Luckily for the child aged one it was decided that his hair had been sufficiently trimmed the day before, else all present would have snipped another lock and placed money into a dish. As it was, the father made a short speech, saying how much had been previously collected, and listing the property now belonging to the infant. It was interesting that with the money they would buy, not a few spare tyres, but some hectares of land.

Mid-afternoon we took our leave. Just as things were really warming up. As if they were there not just to drown their sorrows but to swill them clear of the Andes for ever. A session to banish knowledge and pain. Our last glimpse was of a dancer falling. Flat on the earth. Stunned, asleep.

Next morning I flew back to Lima, through a storm that matched the state of my head. No hawklike feeling on this occasion, but suspense, as if we had been in a tunnel endlessly prolonged for some reason.

Then suddenly the sun over the sea. We swung down towards the city. Smoothly down on to the runway. Back home from a journey to Mars, it seemed. Back home to a Limeñan family.

4

A STUDENT IS SHOT

IT was just after eleven when I reached the street, in a taxi from the airport. Midmorning, cosy in sunshine, the pause before the lunchtime scramble. Meche was standing outside the door talking to a fruit seller, her stomach fractionally diminished. "He will die!" she had been moaning the week before, in penultimate moments; "my life is sorrow." But now she was giggling, she had produced a girl, to be called ingenuously Concepción; she was laughing again with all and sundry.

Inside, the Señora appeared from the kitchen, busy as a mole, her keen glance softening into a most generous welcome. She smiled cryptically over Meche. In reply to my question about Juanita she said I must accompany her there that evening. She offered me a sherry. She sat me down and asked how had it been in the provinces? How had I found Emilio's family? Aware of the cooking smells in the background I knew I must not dally too long; but there was time, unexpectedly, for a profound exchange, as can happen at such moments of arrival before restraints reassert themselves.

It grew out of my enthusiastic comment. I was so relieved to be on the ground again, so glad to be back, that I brimmed over: it was wonderful, wonderful, up in the sierra! Mountain air, monumental views; and the great challenge of this country—to transform the condition of the peasants, etc. Naturally I extolled Huamanga University. Something of that attitude should enter into every young Peruvian's thinking.

She sighed. Then, unexpectedly, "I wish you could convince Roberto of it." Her thoughtful face glowed as if with memories my outburst had recalled; she was regarding the photos of her husband and family, one by one, down to the youngest, this same problematic son. "This is my worry. While his father was alive, he excelled himself in order to please. They planned it together: Roberto would become one of those who open the country, an engineer—perhaps even in the selva, the high altitude jungle, that some of our leaders, like Fernando Belaunde, believe can be the salvation of the South. Of the Indian communities. Of . . . well, you have seen."

She sighed more perceptibly. "Roberto now says he must work in Lima—like everyone. He no longer says what he will do here, though. He is drifting. I am afraid, partly, Carmela is responsible." She broke off, perhaps annoyed at admitting it, as her tone hardened with other thoughts.

"Señora, when I go to the South, perhaps Roberto would like to go with me? The country itself acts powerfully on one."

"You are going there too?" She looked thoughtful, and pleased. Then, "Oh, he will find some excuse for not doing so. His exams! But what exams, I ask. But, tell me, when do you propose to go? I must arrange for you to meet my family—both of my families, in Arequipa, in Puno. Then, Señor, you will understand . . . everything, about Roberto . . . about all of us." She looked sadder again, and suddenly more humble. Her defences were suddenly not there. "You know, I understand him. That is true, too." And smiling, quickening, she was rising from her chair.

Shortly afterwards I went out.

That evening, and on subsequent evenings, I accompanied her to Juanita's. More reserved again she was yet very friendly, enjoying the turns of conversation we had especially on the bus across town. It was soon the norm that I should accompany her and be part of their evening circle; though through the day I kept pretty well clear.

Those were shocking days, shocking in terms of local events; though possibly for the hardened observer, or for the tourist who is always enough streets away, and reads the papers as he might a

novel, assuming he can read the language, they might have been
no more than titillating. They were shocking to Juanita and her
mother.

On the Saturday evening and again on Sunday they went over
what had happened on the Friday. Shortly after noon in the
Plaza de Armas an orderly crowd of two hundred teachers had
been listening to one of their strike leaders: reminding them how
they had waited for a year for the higher pay promised, without
result, so that now they were on strike, some on hunger strike,
but, in accordance with their principles, in peaceable fashion. A
petition had been sent to the President, but so far . . .

At that moment, as if in answer it immediately seemed to their
petition, a water-spraying vehicle had appeared, and a thunderous
jet of water had been launched into the middle of the assembly.
They had run, some up the Cathedral steps, some towards side
streets: but from these had emerged steel-helmeted guards and
squads of the new security police who had bombed them with
teargas and flayed them with long black leather cudgels, a performance that had turned the preliminary amusement of onlookers into fury. "I tell you," said Fernando who had been there,
silently supporting a man he respected, "I tell you, it was a
moment of civil war."

He fell silent again. Here, as at the Señora's, a shadowy figure,
he rarely spoke. His gaze flitted round then returned to stare
inwards, and it was also as if he bled inwardly, persistently, in
some struggle with himself. He was a mechanic's son from a sugar
plantation, owned by another great American company, that
had made possible every step of his studies. The Señora said he
studied too hard, out of a sense of obligation.

The women condemned the police behaviour, and the politicians
who stood behind it, who, they saw, were trying to provoke the
teachers into more militant action: a situation that could at once
be used to justify further repression. "Such an old gambit," said
Juanita, "I've seen it played a dozen times. We all know the
dangers, but tempers fly. It's a war of nerves from now till the

Election. It would be better even to stay trodden under, till then, and keep a cool head."

A student who was present would not have this, and Fernando looked his most wraithlike. Each abuse of justice must be opposed or, history showed it, worse would follow; moreover, while struggling, while demonstrating, the forces of the Left forged their unity, and more of the populace were drawn in. Do nothing in a milksop fashion, and next thing you'd be brainwashed.

This student had a bandaged head. There had been other incidents near the University. He had been smashed up by three policemen.

"Yes." Juanita's radiant gaze clouded with anxiety: she agreed. In fact she had always talked like that, and in Odria's day had worked underground keeping an APRA cell going. But now, so much hung on this Election! Wiser, surely, to go slowly, carefully . . . to keep the field open for responsible change . . . not to play into the hands of violence. Beltran and his crowd were no fools.

"Oh, have you read of his reception in Cuzco! As with Odria in Huancayo, a feast of stones! The people decisively reject Beltran. He has benefited only his own class."

The student exulted. He pressed on swiftly: "We must oppose and discredit him at once. Or else, staying high in America's regard, because he speaks their business men's language, he could be too powerful. I am afraid of it. He could give us a new style of dictatorship." His eyes screwed up with this terrible prospect. He opened his fist, waved it limply, pleading.

The Señora said, "I am certain Belaunde is going to win the next election. It is not just that he comes from Arequipa, but he is a man you can respect. He makes everything clear. He knows every corner of the country, and he is forthright. You know what he said at the Iquitos convention—that if there is not a proper legality, the people will open the doors of force. Now, everyone knows this. Even the Generals. Even Beltran and the other bankers. It is Belaunde who has the following, and they see it is best to leave him to win."

"Oh, I challenge that," began the student, then hushed before the Señora's gaze, glowing and a trifle self-satisfied. Juanita was placidly stroking her tummy. She laughed suddenly. "Mamma, I like to hear you being so dogmatic. Though I fear, when Belaunde talks force, as I was saying a minute ago, he plays the other side's hand. Personally, I have great doubts about him. Isn't he a bit like the Piérola who charmed Peru at the turn of the century? Can we afford another caudillo? As I see it, all his paper plans are subordinate to his personal ambition. Which might mean that the oligarchy see they have nothing really to fear from him. Finally, he wouldn't dare!"

"While Cornejo Chavez on the other hand," she continued, quietly holding the field, "not only again comes from Arequipa" —she smiled winningly at her mother—"but is tougher and more practical, more the one to stick to his party's programme, which is decisively more radical. I believe he is the only man who can avert a Communist revolution—looking ahead a little, that is."

"None of them can!" exulted the student. "They are all playing the middle class game—"

"Juanita," her mother gently chided her, "what is Cornejo but a chip off Belaunde? The one a sapling, the other a tree? And Belaunde is not so old! Wait till he starts his campaign on television. That, my child, will be the revelation of the 1962 election."

Suddenly we were all smiling, at these words rounding off their display of preferences; and as women do, the next moment they had dropped politics as if into a reticule, and were discussing the suitability of one of the Puno uncles, Silvestre Echarri, as godfather for the expected baby. They both seemed to favour the idea: he was the head of the Echarri clan now, with schemes for extending his affairs to Lima; he would make a just and loyal compadre; he might be the one to rescue Roberto. It was this last point, raised by the Señora in such a way that I was allowed to understand it (I could see she had a task for me, too, eventually, with regard to her son), that, the interests of the babe apart, occupied the two women. Roberto, their youngest male, entranced them; his soul must not be lost.

Across a corner of the table the two students had turned to mathematics. Besides encouraging political talk, this household also provided a refuge from threadbare and often lonely lodgings for quite a few young people who were glad of a soup and a place in which to talk over their studies. And not everyone was always talking; sometimes they sat deep in books. Juanita in her simple practicality had something of the Quakeress about her.

On Monday evening, October 23rd, none of the usual faces appeared. There was a compadre there, one Vicente, godfather to the first child, Manuel. Little Manuel who was nearly two seemed always to be rocked in the cradle of the deep, but on this evening he woke up for a moment, and was carried in for inspection. His mother cuddled him and smoothed back the hair from his clear amber forehead: would the next one be so perfect? Then grandmother bore him back to bed. Juanita slumped in a wide-armed chair. The compadre teased her; he was a gay spirit. After the fifth or sixth, he thought, she would have to look for a bigger apartment—only for the sake of the students, of course.

Where were the students?

The compadre had heard of some mammoth demonstration, a protest against last Friday's nonsense. Students were supporting it, but how did you tell who was student and who was teacher when some of these revolutionary types remained in the Faculties until they were forty. And he told us a story about a student who had qualified the same day that he had become a grandfather.

Juanita called him a donkey.

An hour went by; the Señora looked sleepy; then suddenly there was a cry in the courtyard, voices on the stairs, and three students burst in, one of them of the previous evening. Calling on all to listen to their story! To be ready, if this was the moment, to fight! "Señora, you cannot picture the foulness. Do they drink blood, that they need to spill it?" Out of their wild and frightened voices then came the message—a student had been shot. The Congress guard had opened fire, above them, it had seemed, but this youth had fallen. A country youth, just arrived in Lima, a mere fledgeling of a student: but his face had been pulped. And police armed with submachine guns had peppered the surrounding houses, and broken in, and cudgelled any demonstrators taking refuge, and whisked them to prison. This also was the message: Fernando had been caught.

Fernando shot? The Señora was confused, horror and alarm for Juanita's condition, for her daughter had gone a blank white, mixing with her trail of sleepiness. Then she understood. But why had this happened? What sort of demonstration had it been?

The students grew calmer. There had been fiery speeches near the University, but an orderly procession to Plaza Bolivar, to the centre of the square outside the Congress. With the masters, and onlookers, about ten thousand present. They had shouted for the removal of Beltran. But . . . they hadn't got further than that, when again they had been drenched by jets of coloured water from the infernal water machine; then the students had been so incensed they had torn branches off trees and picked up stones and pelted the Deputies' parked cars, and . . . well, that was about all— anger, shouts, a few stones—but in return, bullets. Juan Garcia Collantes shot. "Are they even cynical enough to give us a martyr!" The students looked hard now, and revengeful.

"Where is Fernando?"

But at that moment Juanita in her chair burst into tears. "Go home all of you. We'll see to Fernando tomorrow." The Señora had us out in a minute. We stood downstairs uncertainly continuing. The compadre left; then I accompanied the students back to the centre of the city. There were police everywhere, but also the life of bars and nightclubs, the coming and going of collectivos, in a city that at this point looked undisturbed. There was talk with someone at a street corner. "Would you care to come with us?" I went along, to a school in a street beyond the University, where on a table lit with candles, beneath rough covers, lay the body of the student. That night's work.

Next day the Government issued a decree suspending the right of free assembly.

I was up early and out for the papers. There was a newcomer among them, *Expreso*, hard-hitting and full of news, of radical tone but independent, refreshingly independent of the vendettas that made *El Comercio* and *La Prensa* so tedious. Here was an account of last night's doings; the students had not described it wrong. A single death perhaps was not too shattering from a Latin American point of view; but this one, also perhaps, might prove a milestone. Middle class opinion was solidifying: a cleaner sort of society was called for. Peruanidad, the Peruvian's image of himself, unfakable by any beyond a certain point, was a word I heard often in the following days.

That same evening, returning early to the house, I found the Señora in the sitting room together with Roberto and Carmela. They were calming her down for she was in a rare old state, flushed with extreme annoyance, amazed at some treatment she had received. It took some minutes to sort it out. Her tone was bitter, flustered, stern. She looked equally on edge with her children, and she turned to me as to an older person who would see better into her predicament. In a word, she had failed to rescue Fernando. He was still detained, and who knew by now what the police might have meted out to him; and she herself had been insulted. It was this last she could not really grasp: for though at times in her life she had been insulted, slighted, through following a path of her own choosing, in the old days she had not cared; and she had never once invoked the Montellanos, the last thing she would ever have done, she had never done it . . . from which it emerged that somehow she had done it today. To save Fernando. And it hadn't worked: it was something to do with the man she had talked to after hours in a crowded ante-chamber: he had known her. He had paid a compliment to their father. He had even referred to Emilio's family. He had asked her how many students she boarded. It had become an inquisition. Why? How had he known who she was?

"Because you said you were Carmen Montellano de Echarri," repeated Roberto with extreme distaste. "Mamma, you have always been well known. And remember that other lodger who was a Communist. Do we, now José is doing well, need to continue with questionable students?"

She snapped at him. "We certainly do. If you require the things you require. I will not permit you to live off José. He is already far too generous to us. And these students are not questionable, as you put it: they are unquestionably good simple men. Like Fernando. Who is better than he?"

"He's so shy," murmured Carmela, bored. She was regarding me, for we had so little met that she had not known I was so intimate with the family. To listen like this to bare facts. She was moving herself, with incipient provocation, to show off better her neck and wrists. Roberto noticed her and glowered.

"Mamma," he pleaded, "what now can you do that will not more distress you? Forget it, Mamma. Fernando will return. As he is an American protégé, remember that, nothing can harm him. He's cooling his heels. Come, let's eat something, Mamma."

She sighed, distressed by her son's indifference: couldn't they see where her duty still lay? Was she to take this lying down? Her expression rebuked her half-breed children, and distress at having to do that was part of it: and frankly suddenly I felt it was the core of the state of mind precipitated in her. A Montellano, she was seeing them objectively, perhaps for the first time in years.

Anyway, the next minute she was up ordering Roberto to ring his cousin Carlos, who might still be at the office, to arrange for her to see him. This evening, within the hour, say. She didn't seem to doubt her request would be granted.

Roberto, as if in a strip cartoon, underwent shades of change. His disdain quickened, turned to curiosity. An interested look awoke on his face. He flicked specks off his neat new suiting, that his sister was admiring with covert envy, and went out to telephone. His back, as he walked, was equally expressive: he was already making his best impression.

It was arranged. Naturally he would accompany his mother. He was now, above all, playing the gentleman.

"Ah si," said Carmela, when we were left alone, "you can see the kind of country you have come to. Politics, politics, nothing but politics. Oof! I dislike it." She made a turn, showing off legs, behind, bosom, then very sedately sat down. "We had an American here. Such a nice man. He was a Fulbright scholar, and he complained that his year was being completely wasted. Do you know the States?"

I admitted I did.

"Ah si, it is my ambition to go there. Juanita has been, but what use is it to her? I would settle, I think, in New York, or Chicago. Do you know Texas?"

No, I didn't.

"This American was a Texan. He came from Houston. I was surprised, he was a very lively man. Hombre!"—she was suddenly dissolving in laughter, a minute pause in her speed of talk, like a boat skimming along water—"He was a curious fellow. I wish you could have met him. We don't get enough such visitors in Lima; it is always the same people, and parties, in summer the same faces on the beach. But it is nice to get out of Lima for the day. I and my friends, we go for picnics." She smiled at me, alert and exploratory but still in a very circumspect way. "You must come with us, Señor, one of these days."

I said I should be delighted: for me, too, an unmixed diet of politics was tiring. A few butterfly hours would be a welcome change.

She fastened her quick though offhand gaze more pertinaciously on me. "If only my sister would come out, too, a little more, that would be good for her condition. But she won't!" She dismissed her sister; then, circling round. "You go there every evening, to her flat?"

Yes, but of course I went with their mother.

"Si, Señor, that is understood." She rippled with amusement. Had I made a joke? Her gaze had a curiously penetrating quality, for all its sideways slips and slides. She continued: "I think it must be wonderful to travel across the world. That is freedom. Have you travelled to Spain, Señor?"

Yes, I had lived in Spain once.

"Ah si, my family we have come from Spain. There is still a

part of the estate there. At my cousins' I have seen the family tree, like a great oak—oh, glittering with history! It was a rich family, with many children. Do you spend much time at my cousins' house?"

I reminded her I had just returned from Ayacucho.

"Ah si." She was not interested. She switched on the radio, an explosion of samba, that communicated an extra something to her walk, and she opened a magazine on the table. A commercial started, she changed the station, this time to a mambo, and I thought for seconds, from the increased electricity she gave off, that she was launching into a virtuoso dance; but she switched the set off. She was leaving the room. "Excuse me, Señor, I have friends who are waiting. You will not forget about our picnic?" With an extra flick and daintiness of person she smiled, passed, and had swung from the house.

Meche in the distance started singing again.

Two hours later the Señora returned, satisfied, with Fernando. He had a grisly pallor but was uncommunicative. We all sat down to stew and rice. Roberto too was pleased with himself. As if he had forgotten what had taken them to the office of the eldest son of Esteban Montellano, to the heart of all that millionaire power, he was humming, cogitating aloud, "I think he liked me. Did you notice he asked if I were going to stay in Lima? Do you think I should call on him again, Mamma?"

With our various thoughts we went to bed.

Two days later came a note from Paula: could I dine there on Saturday? I guessed she had heard, round the family tables, of this latest "Echarri manifestation", and had remembered my existence. By now I too pictured her with difficulty.

I went to the house, the high wall in the quiet blossom-petalled street, with some unease. It was so removed from the life I was sharing, not to mentioh the life glimpsed in the sierra, that to accept its hospitality was like a move against conscience. I hadn't realised the degree of my partisanship. I felt suspicious, prickly—not a good dinner mood; so I stopped to buy her a bunch of flowers.

"My dear, how nice—!" That audacious smile, edging through the weight of gloom, her hair this evening in a cleopatra mould, her large body somehow reduced to a more frisky athletic figure. She was immediately again familiar, and sympathetic, though I now placed her socially with the enemy. She gathered this at once. She remarked, "I'm afraid, such tiresomeness I let you in for! Perhaps, I should not . . ." She was pausing as if there were some other family she could think of instead. I said quickly how much I admired the Señora. I said in any case it had been only a detail in a quite fantastic national picture. But I couldn't have wished for a better starting point. "Ah yes, your researches." She absorbed my hostility into a perfectly accommodating manner.

Her husband, Luis Felipe Alvano, was elegant and tall, his Scottish blood enabling him, an obviously supple epicurean, to give a first impression of being stoical. Like her he had a sombre quality, perhaps a mask, for one was suddenly aware of mirth, astute laugher in his eyes. He had great facility for switching the subject, keeping it running along as he chose. I learned later he was expert at bridge. This evening he was a shade preoccupied: he admitted at once it was a difficult moment for a newspaper he partly controlled. As always, the political situation. The paucity of new ideas. The cost of technical improvements. The Americans, for some reason. He had just spent some weeks in New York. What an astonishing city that had become!

Listening to him, one picked up facts, but actually he had told you nothing.

Then the other guests arrived, a lawyer, Villaponte, and his Missouri-born wife whom they all called Mabel. Most of the evening we spoke in English.

The women naturally were paid court to first. Mabel, a character, held the stage, her high drawling college girl voice providing all the cues you needed for good-humouredly laughing at her. She was an utterly transparent person, frolicsome, well-informed, bohemian: tough as nails and glad to tell you any bit of dirt you might not know. She was ventriloquist and doll in one; and I was beginning to learn about Paula's first husband and some obviously enormous skeleton, when Villaponte cut in, even more on the ball, and it was he actually over dinner who assumed the role of prima donna.

He paid elaborate court to Paula. He had a face polished like a billiard ball with a black tuft atop it, his eyes were small, little black points, that gleamed with rhetoric and passion. He extolled the quality of the women of Lima, from their wifely virtues to their impishness, that impishness that had made the tapadas the scourge of travellers and erring husbands. What a jest! What times those must have been! But if we no longer had a Pancho Fierro to portray the Limeña, and the life around her, none the less—a wicked smile at Paula—she was still extraordinary . . . her veiled audacity . . .

One began to think he sought to be her lover.

But it was just preliminary skittles, along with praise for her hair style, the flowers, for a repoussé gold ornament on the mantelpiece, for a land deal Alvano had put through; for it was only after this he found his form with a diatribe against "the middle", the middle as a goal, the middle type of mind, people in the middle—the grey universe. "I abhor your British compromise. You are black or you are white; or else who are you? Who for instance in our country is the half-breed? He is not the aboriginal, the basic worker; he is not the colonist; he is a pitiful mixture. His qualities—laziness, vice, stupidity. Why do you imagine we have social unrest? It's the nature of the half-breed, his misplaced self. He upsets the balance between masters and men, the old natural order in society. It is he who disarranges Peru."

Perhaps I had misheard him somewhere, for even in English he rattled away; but emotionally he was crystal clear and without question one of the masters, free to cavort how he chose; and next minute he was blithely crossing his tracks with "We have nothing to be ashamed of! In so far as there are poor people, they have always been poor, and it is precisely now that thanks to us they are bettering their lot. We, not they, provide the opportunities. Go my dear sir, to the barriadas, our town slums; you will have heard about them. We have nothing to hide; they are a first step out of medieval ignorance to the present. The people there are even to be congratulated; they accept the hand we have held out to them."

"César," said his wife, deep in tournedos, "surely, my love, that . . . ?"

"I assert it. I detest these half-breeds, as I do the Indians; but they are here, in the country, and if they keep their place we can educate them to work and marry. That already will be a revolution." He laughed crisply. "Let them have their revolution! But for the rest, beware. It is we who govern."

"But surely," hummed Paula as though she weren't thinking, "the status quo can never be affected? For your opponents, the law—you know what I mean? Articles 53 and 70, and isn't it 213 also, of the 1933 Constitution? What can anyone do against them?"

"Quite so." In his greed he overlooked her smile, a smile wrapped within her features. "Quite so, Paula, and that is the point I keep making to Luis and his friends—who believe from the electoral point of view that they should still try to combine with APRA. Why? For votes? It is no longer worth it; APRA might bring you thirty per cent. No, I personally have backed Odria—he governed, he kept the state in order—but now I say, better Beltran. Beltran by himself, without alliances. It can't be done? We would need the army? My dear friends, there are times when some manipulation becomes the most patriotic of duties. That is how I approach the Election. Let Haya and Belaunde talk—now. Afterwards . . ." He gestured them into oblivion.

"But wouldn't that bring them into the streets?" I had rashly shoved in my oar again.

"Sir?" His eyes burned, he was a maniac, a cruel smile hovering round the lips. He suggested the lawyer who is brilliant in details, but whose case as a whole is a mess. "And if they do?"

I thought of the student. "But you can't suggest firing on them?"

"Do you imagine they wouldn't fire on us? Look at Cuba. There's your plea for mercy!"

"Oh I guess it's terrible there," said Mabel.

Alvano cut in, "I've heard Beltram is resigning from the Premiership. It could be the finish for him."

"On the contrary, Luis. All this fuss, he retires; but only to return, as I say, to the peak. Throw your support behind him now."

"That unfortunate student!" murmured Paula, but again, subtly, offering bait. Her hand on the table, little movements of her body, suggested she was bored and punishing the feeling, teasing something more excruciating if possible out of the mood this talk induced in her. In a quite different voice she offered more vegetables.

"Unfortunate, Paula?" Villaponte was smoothing the smiling wires of his moustache. "As Catholics, who are we to say? And as for the body politic, such scourgings are the best thing for its soul."

She almost wriggled with her wilful masochism, but it was enough; she led the talk into other fields. We had liqueur soufflé, fruits, coffee. With this, to bite on, bits of scandalous gossip. There was a definite taste for animal details: at these faces lit up.

Then we all went to a nightclub. Alvano drove, a beautiful Mercedes, his blandness and gloved hand on the wheel like an advert for expensive chocolates, as at home, in front of the mantelpiece, he proclaimed only the best of sherries; he saw us in and saw that we were served, then excused himself, to collect some Americans. Paula didn't seem to notice him go. We settled into the dark perimeter, watching the gentle kick of a rumba, and the antics of the band singing snippets, encouraging the dancers, enticing others with cries and comment as if we had been in a giant aviary. The rhythm quickened. More movement of shoulders, bosoms, hips, feet. A general swivelling of behinds; the machine-like grace of so many mincers on a kitchen bench. Society girls, aspiring matrons, hostesses, others: all seemed gifted with the knack of these tremendously concupiscent movements. Hands pawed the air, feet trod, while the flesh in between swivelled and shook; faces laughed, or perhaps talked of the weather, for this was native ground for mambos, and it all happened as easily as breathing.

Villaponte eyed it playfully, an expression that made him look more sinister, then he lit a cigar. His wife was prattling. I suggested to Paula we join the dance.

"That's more refreshing." My lead was subdued relative to the other practitioners but she made up for it, her tall moody body gyrating as if her life depended on it. She was shaking out the evening's boredom. Then she settled into a more restrained movement, closer, infinitely more provocative. But why not provoke? This was the dance. Her brooding face was lit with mischief. It was a very pleasurable game to play. "A new field for your researches. Or is this ruled out?" We laughed, for there was a reciprocal sympathy. The rhythm had become a pointed illustration to what one could not help but feel. On and on, the insistent drummer playing the nerve strings of his puppets. Even though not a Latin American, eventually one was caught up in it, as freely moving as anyone else. No wonder from every hour of the radio ticked out these liberating currents. Mambo the teacher of us all.

Then after a pause came a dreamy blues. Circling like fish in a phosphorescent pool, soothed, lubriciously in contact. The floor space filled with would-be dreamers. Paula, always a thought ahead, smiled at a set of possibilities. "I think," she said, "we had better go back. Villaponte is looking jealous."

He did look nasty. Then Alvano came, with two studiously polite Americans, and the evening proceeded differently. We watched an average cabaret. For some reason it amused Paula, taking a risk, to hold my hand. But dancing again, she had become aloof, dissociated from our actions. They had peeled off her. They had not been. She was so strong a character, and the deed so slight, that it was obviously best to leave it at that. But she had lost that mambo look of contentment.

She was back in her over-complicated world.

We were all soon back in the black Mercedes, that like some timeless symbolic chariot bore us through the sleeping city. When they dropped me I watched it receding down the street. The illusion it conveyed clung for a time. I fell asleep dissatisfied.

But morning reasserted realities, homely, easier on the conscience. Being a Sunday they were all there. The Señora was fretting over Fernando, who for the last three days had dropped his studies, and was interested only in playing cards. He and Roberto were having a game. Carmela was in and out of the bathroom, waiting for friends to pick her up. Meche was hushing babies in the kitchen.

"To change the world," said the Señora, tying on a scarf to go to Mass, "one must first work with the world. It's a hard lesson, I know, Fernando. I beg you, don't give up your studies."

"Si, Señora, I will try again."

She turned to me, in an access of relief, and invited me to eat with them at midday, as it was a Sunday.

Bedrock.

5

LOW LIFE

Settling more into the Señora's round didn't mean only serious discussion and left-wing politics. There was Carmela. Intoxicated by his new French lotion, there was Roberto. Though they too and as seen by themselves had individual problems, and, more curiously, what they hid from themselves, they had inclinations that seemed to derive from the coarser blood within them. Their stability was delicately poised. They were seldom two days the same. They used up so much energy trying to be something they didn't quite match. And of course seeing Juanita, who occasionally appeared at her mother's house for they never went to her apartment, and feeling her serenity, they were vexed. They were jealous. They quarrelled with their mother. And more than ever they set themselves to follow the American-type modes of the capital.

So that to be in their company was rather like wandering on to the set of a bad play. Artifice abounded, then bursts of frankness. They parodied themselves, retreated, sulked. They wooed your attention, cut you dead. Styles were hopelessly confused.

That same Sunday Roberto suggested taking me to watch the great annual procession of Señor de los Milagros, but tired of the idea even as he spoke it; so that I went with Fernando, and we saw very little except for the usual sporting crowd, the pockets of hysteria and exhibitionism, the tawdry pomp of bygone times; but we did bump into Carmela and her friends, who had decided against their planned outing and were going to someone's house to dance. "We're having the picnic on Wednesday," she announced; "perhaps you are free to join us then?" She deftly

excluded Fernando, who, a pace away, pretended not to hear.
Carmela's friends were good looking, fastidiously groomed, and
white in skin tone. Beside them her tan showed darker. She
continued pressing me to join them as if to show off how well she
knew me. I had already accepted. She urged me again. Momentarily, I was an exhibit.

Wednesday was a religious holiday in honour of the dead.
People went to Mass and to cemeteries. Since Sunday there had
been further demonstrations, and douchings from the water
machine, in honour of the student Collantes, but today people
turned to their families, draped in black they crowded to the
graves and sprinkled holy water on their ancestors. The cemeteries
sang with flowers. The Señora looked set for the day, but after
Mass Carmela was free, and by midday six of us were bowling
out of Lima in an ancient Chevrolet. Typically, we had been
going to the beach, but on impulse turned about to the mountains.
There were wooded walks near Chosica, and a small restaurant.
That was now the plan.

Once out of the car and walking in sunshine, there was a burst
of excitement and the usual frolics of town dwellers for their
first hour in the country. Everything in view was delicious.
Orchards. A waterfall. A tumbled nook. The great blanket of
mist beyond us, covering Lima and the coastal desert. Above, the
scaly peaks were noted, and the wonder of Peru's geography, as it
must have been each time they came here; even they talked of
exploring further, to Cuzco or Iquitos, as tourists sometime.

Then we sat down, still thrilled by the view, at a terrace table
and began to eat. Wine from the district of Ica to drink. Cebiche,
egg soup, prawns, chicken cooked in onion and aji (the really
fierce pepper of the coast), goat cheese, and coffee. From the
radio, criollo waltzes. Beside Carmela and her friend, Santiago,
there was Osman, a half-German boy, and his friend Vicky, a
buxom blonde with long sleepy hair to her shoulders, then Macú,
short for Maria de la Cruz, a dark shy hollow-faced girl who had
already been to Europe, and so, smiled Carmela, "Is a little like
you no? She has travelled". She was pleased at having produced

Macú. Macú came of richer parents, wore slightly finer clothes, was studying vaguely. Carmela kept encouraging her to show off. Among friends it improved the occasion if each one boasted a bit.

After some glasses of wine this worked. Macú was really a sweet girl, ready to oblige anyone; her shyness faded, a titter broke forth, she fiddled with her pearls and a gold bangle, and began, much prodded and abetted by Carmela, to relate her experiences in England. "You see, I had a friend, who after a month"—there were hoots of laughter at the word "month"— "no, no, you are too quick, there was nothing like that!"—their laughter now nearly unseated them—"listen to me . . . my friend, this boy—no, listen, please, or I won't go on . . ." She too was tittering compulsively. "All that happened was that he took me to his home and his father said 'I've made a cake! For you, I've made a cake for your visit!'"

What! They couldn't understand exactly.

"His father, the man, had made a cake!"

"Oh!" They all roared. I did too. I said: "Yes, in England today the husbands often help their wives. According to their abilities."

"Yes, yes." Encouraged, she was now pouring it forth. "And after tea when I stood up, you know, just to stretch my legs, he hastened to say 'Don't offer to help! I shall do the washing up later.' A man!"

They were convulsed. I put in feebly, "We don't have servants in England, like you." They didn't hear me. "What else? What else?" They were refilling her glass. Keep it up, Macú. She said, "Yes, the prams. On Sundays in the parks men pushing the prams. I could not get used to that."

"No, in Peru, men are men, after all . . ."

"Worst luck, sometimes—"

"But what about the boy? The English boy. Did he kiss you?" Macú coloured and calmed down.

"Oh, you've spoiled it," cried Carmela; "naturally he kissed her. But Macú, was it different in Spain?"

"Completely different. More like here. But not like here, it was more hypocritical—"

"Impossible!" they all shouted at once.

"Yes," said Macú, "and someone asked me, 'Are you from Peru? How well you speak Spanish! Have you been studying it very long?'"

They laughed more cynically at that. "Those Spaniards," said Osman, "they're so old-fashioned. They know nothing. They think we're all millionaires. But a Spanish student I met in Lima told me he envied our freedom here. In Madrid it's stifling."

"Oh?" They didn't care. Santigo and Osman worked in offices, and Vicky in the same bank as Carmela. They looked for money, security, status. They wanted to have a good time. As Carmela said a minute later, "I shall marry only a very rich man. I shall stay in bed till eleven, si, and have five, six maids for the children, go to parties—"

"You go to parties now."

"Yes, but every night in my new life. Bridge parties for the afternoons. I shall have a Sambo as a chauffeur, and wear mink. I'm only teasing, Santiago, hombre." Santiago's scorn had turned a bit green. "You think it's wrong to like money, no?"

"We almost thought you had become an American." Osman was a trifle heavy in his teasing.

"Caramba!" Then she decided not to be teased. "Not an American, muchas gracias, like the one who owns Santiago's company. He's mean. Some of these Americans are mean. They are so rich, they look down on you. Toof! I tell you, they lack personal feeling. If you're late, you are not feeling too good, they say, 'Hey! Twice late. Here are your cards.' No give, no heart. Falta corazon." She acted it as if it had happened to her. "Isn't it, Santiago, amigo?" She was jogging him into a smile again. He was one of the touchy cavalier type.

"It isn't so easy," she continued, still serious, "these days in Lima. What are people like us to do? The price of meat, it's impossible. So are clothes. Do you want me to buy Peru-made clothes?"

"Yes, of bayeta cloth! I can see you, in six bright skirts and a bowler, the baby slung in a shawl behind, coming from market!"

It was Carmela's turn to blush. Osman had said the worst thing possible. He tried to retrieve it, "Miss Peru! Once again we could win the Miss Universe prize." Santiago tried, "Peruvian materials are now equal to anything being imported. Don't let's be snobs."

It was no use. Carmela, her tan overlaid with red, almost startled into tears, was not to be comforted. Her day was smashed. Her aura of dreams.

We paid. We strolled through the woods. They discussed a murder and a television show. The murderer, for Carmela, was a pig. He was dirty, sucio, an ignorant beast. It was easy to gather he was in fact a countryman, an Indian who had not adjusted to Lima. She worked off some of her irritation. Then she laughed at the memory of the TV show. "We're getting a TV set," she boasted.

"Are you?"

"Si. I've decided we must do." She began to feel much better now. "Roberto will arrange it."

On this high note, which she was allowed to hold, we rattled happily back to town. They sang recent song hits. They talked of friends, pulling their unfortunate characters to pieces. They discussed the coming summer on the beach. Soon we were back in the blanket of mist. All except Macú could go to the cinema. So I dropped out too.

Arriving home I found Roberto, in a brittle mood, looking for trouble. Till now he had maintained towards me the careful courtesy of a man about town; but something had gone wrong with his day. His mother had obliged him to accompany her, then had returned not here but to Juanita's. Meche was back with Serafino, the policeman, and though she mattered little to the young master, it was one more scratch to his pride. He disliked outings to the country, and I don't think he had many friends; he had quarrelled often, and he tired of people. His one consuming interest was women; but today he was interested in no one.

I had actually thought the house was empty. It was more than just silent, it gaped with silence. Doors stood ajar, dusk was filtering out of the rooms and up the stairway. I had letters to write but I fancied a soft drink, and I had been given permission to help myself if no one else was there to do it, so I went to the kitchen and took a coke from the fridge, and came to the sitting room to drink it.

He was slumped in a chair, staring furiously.

I apologised at once; I had not known he was there.

"If you had done, would you have helped yourself, freely, from our kitchen?"

Certainly, his mother had given me permission.

"Ah yes. It has been arranged. By her." His tone seethed with envy and frustration. "You are a rich man. You obtain your desires. Though I do not know what you want with us here?"

"Look, Roberto, don't speak like that. It is offensive to me." Twice his age and probably as strong I was quite ready to punch his nose. He laughed shortly but shut up. I went to my room.

He followed in a while. A knock at the door. "I apologise, Señor, for my words to you." His tone had become icily contemptuous. "But my curiosity about you remains. It is only natural, as you have 'joined' our family, to seek for explanations." He was cold, ironic, then he began to wheedle. He was being caught by his need to know.

I said, "I'm studying colonial history, so as to be able to write about it. The rest of your family don't find this strange. At this point, really, I ought to be in Cuzco, but I find Lima so attractive. I shall be off soon. Would you care to come with me?"

"I?" He was quick. "My future lies here." But he was suddenly more sociable, and then a bit impudent. "Perhaps it is my sister whom you find attractive? You had a pleasant outing today?" His teeth gleamed in an even row.

"Of course. We went to the hills near Chosica. Everybody talked and sang. Limeñians talk rather fast, though, for me. I miss all the current slang."

"Huachafa." His smile continued evenly. "That's old slang, but it fits Carmela. Like cursi in Castellano. Pretentious. Did she talk about high society to you, la alta sociedad?" He was agleam with spite. "You should see her walking when she leaves the office, round Jiron Union. Like a putana. Who has she caught, though? I advise you, don't touch Carmela." He was waving his sister out of each.

He came back to other possibilities, "So you are not here for a business firm, or in the interests of your Government? Just for study?" He nodded with amazement, but he was by now losing interest. "Señor John, we are friends. My house is yours for as long as you may need it. Shall we go out for a drink together?"

So we wandered about for the rest of the evening. Nothing really pleased Roberto. He was busy with secret trains of thought, and on the surface criticising what he saw. It was just three weeks since I had first met him, but already he looked a fraction slacker, more dependent on some desperate solution. He was disinclined to talk about himself, but spoke worlds through his comment on others.

We drifted towards the classier bars, which he didn't for any reason prefer—in fact, at some level anxious on account of his clothes and skin colour, he would have avoided them if it hadn't been for the chance of an amatory encounter. He had no anxiety on that score. He accosted whomever he liked with a smile, a gesture, a compliment. His eyes shone, his face composed itself into one of easy mastery: he attacked. The women liked it and in turn put up the accepted barriers of defence. They ignored him, or returned a phrase calculated to spur him further, or in one case very simply complied and made a date for the cinema tomorrow. That was in the street and in a bus we took; in the bars, as all the women had protectors, his tactics were more snake-like. He wasn't always determined on a conquest, but to start things off was compulsive with him.

In one bar, an obvious front window for the discreeter type of prostitute, he proposed we take a couple and he seemed to be proposing I should pay for them both. I declined. He pursued the theme. He knew one or two excellent houses. We should go by taxi as they were outside the centre. "I have to think about you," he explained. "It is unpleasant for you to go so long. Or have you, amigo, found someone?" I confessed I had not. "So

then it is settled? If you don't like whores, I will arrange some girl.
In the next street there lives a widow. I and all my friends have
gone with her. This has nothing to do with morality, Señor; you
are a man, still in the prime of life. It must happen."

This theme so cheered him that as by now we had arrived in
the Plaza Dos de Mayo, he proposed a visit to Tropicana, the big
popular music hall, staged as far as I could see under canvas,
where nearly all the acts were provided by performers from the
provinces. It was a fiesta of reunion. Friends greeted friends.
Countrymen still feeling strange in Lima regained the simpler
modes of the sierra; they went wild when a three-piece band and
a singer from their very own district appeared. Huaynos,
pasacalles, mulizas or yaravís, serrano waltzes: the music of the
mountains, of processions and of love, of ritual and soliloquy
recreated that world around them, that lost world for these city
settlers. The musicians wore the traditional costumes and played
flutes and drums, and sometimes lutes and guitars; and then for
those from the coastal valleys there were creole waltzes, polkas,
marineras, light as froth and teasingly gay; then back to the
stamp and the trip around of the unendingly repeated huayno.
The flutes held the melody, the tambors beat; the singer told of
war and love, then, peak of excitement, a girl appeared, or two
or more, and danced about the stage, flirting coquettishly with
the singer. They flirted with us all. We were caught up in the
rhythm, stamp, stamp, swing about and round: "otra vez",
"mas", more, cried the audience, and from time to time a man
jumped up, lean or plump it didn't seem to matter, and left his
seat and climbed on to the stage and joined in the performance.
"He comes from the same village!" cried Roberto; and Roberto
by now was lost in excitement.

Suddenly he couldn't hold back any longer. I think it was
simply the very pretty dancer. He shot up there, and was twirling
around her. He was an adroit, a magnificent partner, "Vaya!"
at first the audience cried, but then "Bravo! Un serrano,
legitimo!" They acclaimed him as a true-born countryman. They
roared when they saw he was intriguing the girl. He was

unquestionably getting something across to her. It became the high spot of the evening.

He was in his own element all right.

But afterwards outside he disparaged it. "I learned it at school. I prefer to samba, naturally." Indifferently, he dismissed the incident.

Fernando was becoming more friendly. His suspicions very pronounced at first at having a gringo in the house had gone. In part he took his cue from the Señora, and the fact that I was now invited to eat with them on a Sunday settled the issue. He began to pass me thoughtful rather obscure ideas from some unending cogitation of his own, gleaned, to judge by the terminology, from a philosophical manual of a century ago, and he popped questions on the outer world, on Sweden and Ghana and the division in Kashmir, even on the merits of the Rolls Royce engine, always in his shadowy deprecating way, and whatever the answer it was carefully fed into his mental process. He was a dedicated student. He had to keep the wheels of knowledge grinding.

In return he taught me El Rocambor, an innocent card game with a Spanish pack, at which Roberto sometimes joined us; though Roberto preferred poker, and to gamble, or to scintillate round a billiard table.

My last Saturday, as it turned out, in Lima before returning to the mountains, Fernando suggested I should accompany him on a visit to a friend of his, also from the north, from the coastal basin of sugar plantations bordering Trujillo, who like so many young people had migrated here, seeking work in the El Dorado they all imagined the capital to be, but who was forced to live in a slum area off the Avenida Grau. He had found only casual labour. His appearance had deteriorated, he could no longer get commissions selling from door to door. He had worked in the meat market, then clearing land. For some time he had not worked at all. A girl he lived with kept him going.

"His family and mine were neighbours. Our fathers are

compadres. He is my close friend. But there was no work for him on the estate, and he had ambitions. I do not see what else he could have done, but it is a living death for him in Lima."

"He's in one of the barriadas?"

Fernando's expression retreated behind an oblique smile. "Yes, he is. It is not where foreign journalists are taken, in Fray Martin de Porres. Nor near El Montón, the city dump, where a year ago human beings and pigs fought together for scraps of food. There has been publicity—that is one of the features I note as conducive to evolution; in consequence, some remedial measures. But there are shack towns on either side of Lima, stretching into the desert, flimsy but, as it never rains, secure; and they have air there. Here, I propound, you will meet something worse."

"Doesn't it make you see red? Side by side with the millionaire suburbs? The people who bribe their way out of taxes, who keep two, three villas to a family?"

He frowned thoughtfully. "I do not know. Yes, I know, I mean I know it is wrong. But I wish to say that I distrust revolutions. I am not a 'Red'." He said the word in English. "I distrust the people who cry the slogans; they are usually as bad. I stand with Emilio: we must solve this technologically, through education and scientific method—through planning. Well I see then, yes, I am a Socialist. But I do not like political emotions."

"But if your Government holds you down by force? If it avoids rational solutions, and defends the wealth of two per cent of the people? You, after all, have encountered the police?"

He pondered. "I really do not know. I believe, like Emilio, in world opinion. The Alliance for Progress can be a great lever. Our terrible situation must change—I see; but I see too that it is all the time changing. There was a time when the peasants knew nothing, when they turned their backs to the modern world. Today—it is the impact of the aeroplane, those first flights across the cordillera: you see, evolution, not revolution—they send their children to rural schools, put savings into credit co-operatives, they buy tractors, trucks; they organise their labour. Their children will qualify for the vote. Nothing can halt this rate of advance. By itself, I am sure. But I also see that North America will assist it. There, too, there has been a change of outlook."

"You think there will be time?"

"Time is an elastic conception, I think. I read of it in a book by Bergson. Er . . ." He had forgotten, but began happily ransacking the elastic store-room within his mind. Our bus was heading up the Avenida Grau, a main artery towards Chosica, past institutions, car repair yards, break-up yards, stacks of tyres and other car parts, abandoned vehicles, anonymous walls, and side streets of low dwellings all crushed together like so many villages packed up and delivered here. Grime and disrepair marked them all. It was a poor, a well-known thieving quarter. We got down just before San Cosme and penetrated to the yard we sought.

A high-walled narrow entrance, with a balcony above and dingy doorways. Children's faces, smells, clatter. Then beyond, a space roughly equivalent to a suburban villa's back lawn, of cobbles, fouled earth, debris, with near to the pump a few hens pecking and more children playing among them, and about this, badly cracked from tremors and never repaired, all sagging down, a two-tier and then a one-tier building with doorways each of which opened on a dwelling, a single room without a window, and the other two sides made by a wall with wood shacks leaning to. Even here, a hierarchy of sorts; though the bad odours and the bad light had to be shared by all.

Fernando's friend lived in a room in the single tier section with his girl, and other members of her family, about ten of them in all. They were negroes. She herself was ravishing, a sparkling face with long earrings, a protuberant body, a clean tight dress. Their corner with its bed was curtained off, but it could not have been easy for them. We came in like visitors from Mars, Fernando, the poor student, like a lord; and very welcome we were made, with bright glances and overflowing laughter, but then Fernando had to answer questions that reduced him almost to incoherence. This friend of his had an Indian face with a long arrogant Roman nose, pocked cheeks, unflinching eyes, and a lean loose lazy body. He wanted to know about Fernando, his studies, his future with the American company that owned the estate and their families' lives up there near Trujillo. How did it feel to be specially gifted, to have been picked, cared for, marked for success? Fernando might rise to run the laboratory, might even one day become a manager. "Tell me, Fernando," he seemed to be saying, "how does life feel from your side?"

And Fernando who with half of himself worked blindly at his studies, and with the other half groped for rational understanding but was never finally settled with it, began to wilt, to sweat thinly as the blood inside him ebbed away. He was in anguish. He brought out answers mechanically. He could not find the starting point of any of his usual sets of ideas.

He was used to keeping himself out of it.

This friend had a soft smooth voice, recapitulating the past. "It was when they replaced the cane cutters with machinery. That showed us where we got off. It didn't affect my father, or yours, but the whole system changed. For the better. I know you think so, Fernando—for the better! The Unions have pushed up production, we benefit. Modernisation must come. I accept it. But why are half the young people out of work, derelict there, as if on an island? Who is responsible for those lives, cut off, as on each of those little plantation kingdoms, from the rest of our country? I am speaking of Peruvians. Who is it who controls their lives? Where is that power finally located?"

"Baldo, it is a very progressive company. The hospital, the new houses built . . ." Fernando halted; began again, "We cannot blame them for the number of our children. In every Department now of Peru . . ." He appealed. But this was not yet the issue. He said, "Peruvian owners are worse . . . I do not understand you, Baldo. More young people must leave, perhaps."

The friend smiled his soft sad smile, with his bitter pride of person behind it. "Yes, more must leave. All must leave. That is the answer I wanted, amigo. All must walk out of those private kingdoms, however well run they are. That is the first step of manhood. You do not understand me, Fernando, but even if I don't eat today I feel free in this city barriada, here in the capital of my country, open to all quarters of the earth. I am my full height here. I breathe." He began acting it.

"Baldo, mio, no one breathes in this sewer!" The girl friend was caressing his arm. "We find you a job. We get out of here. Have a little house, a car, maybe. You're sure you couldn't get a job on that estate? Why did you leave your family, caro? Some other girl trouble there?" She was pinching his arm, smiling contentedly. They lay back, staring at Fernando.

Fernando said it was time to go. He looked completely paralysed.

We did the return jouney in silence, and separated at Plaza San Martin. I had letters to post, and he went home. I could only hope the Señora would help him, and tell him that his friend was envious.

I posted my letters at the Hotel Bolivar, a very satisfactory post office, and wandered out the other way through the lounge. I looked at the table where the day before I had given Macú tea and Paula a drink; now it was taken by an elderly couple whose expressions proclaimed that all was vanity. I was just elaborating comparisons, when I saw Azuarga, unexpectedly framed by the cake trolley, a bevy of fancy girls, and two trans-world Americans. He was with the Americans. He was getting up, leaving. I caught him by the door. "Compadre, you here?" I thought I might **as** well tease him.

He guffawed, fiercely embraced me in Latin American fashion, and pulled me into the square. He signalled a taxi. "Come, you go with me. We are off to watch a football match. Or they are all dancing, or drunk by now!" He bundled me in and twisted after, and began a rapid exchange with the driver.

"Drunk footballers?"

"Something else! The most interesting feature of our city life. And at the same time equally a feature of the most distant country districts. The link between—their clubs here. Hundreds of clubs, do you see: links. This one, for instance, is of a district—no, it is the second of that district, for they always splinter—to the south-east of Ayacucho. Also, there are village clubs in Lima, if the village has say a thousand inhabitants; and Provincial and Departmental clubs for the well-to-do and politicians. But this one, or perhaps there are two today—I was forgetting, there is this football match—is, well, I will explain it to you later. What have you been up to . . . compadre? And why aren't you back in the sierra? Or else you'll really experience the rains. Ay!"

We talked a bit, and then I noticed that we were heading up Avenida Grau. "But I've just come from here." I told him about Fernando and the friend and their private company estate back-ground. Azuarga pinned on Fernando. "He talks of inevitable change? Quite true. But possibly, can it not change for the worse? Our population grows at three per cent per annum. That means, in the sierra, every year, an additional hundred thousand souls. But there are already at least a million too many by anything above a scavenger's standard. When I was young they died from disease—you could enter a village and in every house some child under five was succumbing; today, it's hunger. Each year they're more hungry. That's what the affluent mind must grasp. Why do you imagine they trail down here? Oh yes, true, there's glamour!"

Savage, his face veritably contorted, he prodded me with his finger. "Please! Go to Cuzco and to Puno. Now. Take your camera, and your notebook, and get back to the sierra. See that what I say is a mere prologue. Prologue to the basic facts about Peru. Get to know, if you can, the peasant. Then come back here and I'll tell you the rest, about inflation and the price of foreign investment, about rich Peruvians who ought to be investing but prefer to lock their money in Switzerland. Your chum believes in the Americans. Splendid! But what will happen if we socialise, if we go for strictly Peruvian priorities? What happened in Mexico once, in Guatemala, Venezuela, Cuba? Whose cheap backyard are we?" His laugh was harsh, he was rigid with passion. If a

man like Villaponte had been present he would doubtless have
ground him to dust on the spot.

How then, between such people, avert conflict?

He returned to Fernando. "His excellent company will certainly do very well for him. I bet he told you about the hospital.
Which is something up on a neighbouring estate that provides
only thirty sick beds for its seven thousand workers. But if your
chum were politically active and wanted to bring in, say,
Belaunde, an irreproachably decent man, as a change from church,
cinema, socials, into the plantation's main piazza, to talk to them
about their country: could he? To whom do these workers'
minds belong? And his and its sister company are progressive.
You should see some of the estates—prisons! You must let me have
a chat with Fernando. Up that coast, with the population exploding, there is a classical Marxist situation."

He looked smug suddenly, savage but smug, busy with adroit
calculations. I knew I must not deliver Fernando. I asked,
"Which party do you belong to? And who is going to win the
Election?"

Azuarga grimaced. "I sit on the fence. To make sure that when
they send me to prison it will be for the most deserving cause.
And I can tell you who will not win the Election . . . the people
we are joining now. Look! Here we are."

A serrano club. A football field behind a school, ringed by
slum streets just off the Avenida, a crowd of something less than a
thousand, not counting the watchers from the school wall, two
bands playing to encourage the footballers, but there was so much
shouting and general noise, much of it round the refreshment
marquees, that already the effect was of growing disorder, the
game about to give way to stampede. "Que hombre!" The great
thing, at this amateur level, was for each player to show his
prowess, as if turn by turn they were doing a fandango, to get the
girls acclaiming him. Cries. A goal! The bands trumpeted. Only
a few more minutes to go. The surge towards refreshments
thickened. The crowd, to my surprise, were dressed in city style,

there were only a few old women who looked the part of serranos come to town, but my mentor explained, "That is the point. Adaptation to the city, to the national culture: that is why these clubs sprang up, and their influence reaches back to the villages, preparing each wave of emigrants. They adapt, they also give solidarity, and a chance for a countryman to be himself for a few hours of an evening if he needs it. No coastal people, costeños, to sneer at him. He can talk to his fellows, eat his own food. Meet the sort of girl he trusts. He can also combine to push his village interests, right into the office of the Minister concerned. In a club like this, a district club, he can also hope for a small leg up from someone higher in the social scale. It's more democratic than in the sierra. And he'll probably end, if he's important in the club, by returning to be important in the village. Of course, there's plenty of scrapping too."

We pushed round the crowd. Azuarga was looking for the man who had invited him to come along. We were into the midst of the clamour and the music. Some young braves were already dancing. Some of the girls were extraordinarily lovely, their fresh brown skin and clear wide eyes, their abundant black hair enhanced by the change from shawls and straw hats to European modes. They were ripe and wonderfully at ease with the men, equals at this stage of the game. The drinking round the marquees was serious and no one was standing out of it. That total involvement in a good spree, Andean scale, was under way.

We found our contact as the game ended. The surge for a moment almost pushed us through a tent, through vats of chicha and potato stew; a tornado seemed to be coming our way; then it veered, and as two more bands joined in, the company flowed back to the field. Each corner became a dance floor, four separate dancing areas, but the ensemble was like a ballet finale. Stand on a chair, to see this twirling congregation, and the whole of Lima seemed to be spinning, stamping, advancing and retreating to the huayno. Here was a strength to move mountains, and right inside the citadel.

6

THE DEEP SOUTH

NEXT week I flew down to Arequipa. We followed the thin coastal strip between the mountains and the sea. Most of it was desert, grey and yellow, with a burgeoning of orchards and sugar and cotton fields wherever a river cut across, like a succession of little Egypts. The highway dotted with trucks and cars and long distance collectivos gleamed like a metal rod beneath us, disappeared in haze, returned round a headland where the cool foam beckoned one down, then thrummed across the wastes again. By road the journey took eighteen hours, by plane less than three; and I had been warned that to go by collectivo was to court disaster at every bend. Though next month when I went to Trujillo by road, up the continuing strip to the north, I found the collectivos not only very safe, but so fast, swooping like birds to their prey, breaking like a clarion call into one settlement after another, that even more than in the planes I felt to be participating in a great countryside awakening. Transport, movement, further horizons: all this was a key to contemporary Peru.

The desert rose, and the plane curved inland. Ravines, a billowing of scrub, and at seven and a half thousand feet we came to the oasis of Arequipa set at the foot of three volcanoes. A sizeable oasis, no more than that, for the sand and the rubble pressed against and even reappeared in the checkerboard of green. In powerful sunlight we banked steeply and came with a bump on to the runway.

An hour later I was sitting in the office of the Señora's brother, Augusto Montellano. Dusty and spiky as Spain outside in the hot square before the Cathedral it was chilly in the shade of his lawyer's rooms. An aloof establishment, leather bound, the clerks with sharp sad faces, it immediately toned down the effect of the upland air upon one's system. Waiting, one began to feel restless, inhibited, not able to sit there much longer; I wanted to be up and frisking about, inhaling the air from those snowy volcanoes; but I had to conform to the austere pomp I could see was a bridle about this city. Down there in the square, the centre of a pattern that was a replica of every Spanish town, there was neither the pullulating bustle of Lima nor the dazed squalor of Ayacucho: there was pride, address, the tension of memories. The women looked handsome and of upright carriage, rather as if they had stepped down from portraits, or they were peasant women plodding through, eyeing hungrily on either side, or they were schoolgirls, tenuously modern. The men looked quiet, inbred, suave. There were police standing beside the stones still tumbled down from some recent earthquake. There were clerics. There was a middling pace. It was as if one were actually watching a scene from one or two decades before.

"Señor?" Augusto Montellano appeared and drew me into his sanctum, heaped high with volumes and documents. His grave decidedly haughty bearing warned one on no account to beg. Firmly though with a natural grace he saw me seated, glanced at a paper, then looked briskly at the wall above me as though he had thought of another reason why I was certainly wasting his time. He must have read his sister's letter, that, together with my card, I had sent in to him; but it was not enough. He was of middling size, fleshy, flushed; a man perhaps used to riding his estates and those of his more important clients, where, over a suitable repast, he took a stand on innumerable issues. This office, more than his, was his family's cloister; ancestral learning cloaked the walls. There were old engravings, certificates, titles, yellowing in their frames. In the second's pause before we spoke whole centuries yawned away.

However, as soon as I had mentioned Paula, her father, and other introductions that by now I had accumulated, for my last days in the capital had been a whirl, he expanded into somebody

quite different, or, at least, startlingly complementary. Todo o
nada. It was now todo. He was still the seignior, but pocket by
pocket he revealed unexpected largesse. He was solicitous for
my stay in their city, entertainments came into view; the adjoining campiña, the countryside, his nearest vineyard for instance at
Vitor, or Jesús or Socosani for the waters, was worthy of an afternoon's drive. Professor Toynbee had been here last year. Arequipa
was for the refined palate. The stone carvings on La Compañia.
Many old families to meet.

Not a word more was said about his sister, but I could not but
suspect that the emotion contained within these successive
flourishes had less to do with snobbery than with her. She was
centrally ensconsed within the smiles wavering to and fro.

We were interrupted. The phone rang. Señor Augusto tapped
his desk, interlarded some rounded comment, then began to rant
at high speed, following the instrument to the left and up, worry-
ing it with indignation. He subsided. He pronounced judgment.
Proud and magisterial. Then he rang for a clerk.

Minutes later, having been sent for, another man entered from
some other room. He was short, gross, a big-eared fellow, with a
rasping utterly untrustworthy voice. His side look, the whiskers,
the cunning cheeks, suggested even now he was dissembling with
his master. But he must have his uses; he was a political stooge. I
had gathered from the phoning that there had been a setback in
the collection of signatures for some local candidate. A transport
Union had been recalcitrant, and worse, some Montellano
minions. Señor Augusto himself would tackle them. But first,
the stooge must pave the way.

There was a feeling in the room of heads to be broken, of
awkward chaps to be taught a lesson.

Then the stooge was dismissed, and sweet order returned. My
host was offering me a whisky. His language regained its grave
geniality. He invited me to dinner that evening. He would be
honoured to discuss England with me, for his son Jorge—"we
often call him George", and now my host spoke the soft singing
English I was encountering among Peruvians—was studying

there to be a railway engineer. Arequipa was a centre of British railwaydom. The town was indebted, work was provided; and for his son, he had been assured, there would be a good career.

We parted shortly after and I spent the day reeling from the strong mountain air. I examined the churches, a museum, the British Institute, and various small picanterias, eating booths where the food was sharp; and in the Institute looking at *Vogue* and sipping the pisco sours that that establishment's barman was adroit at producing I had the sudden feeling that this place was Bath—no, Bath moved to the Costa Brava, or even to the extreme south of Sicily: no, that again was wrong, for how explain the air, that made one even groggier than pisco. It had this other quality of making one itch, indolent and quicksilver restless by turns. By midday I had procured my ticket onwards, for the Puno train of the following night, on to the Señora's other family. But slow, there was still the one here to meet.

Señor Augusto collected me in the evening, in a very fine car that was like a box at the theatre as we purred through the evening display in the streets. Those tantalisingly pretty girls that appeared only to disappear, from office or shop into shop or cinema, or here to be whisked away by their parents; then lighted booths, the Cathedral steps, the men sauntering through the arcades. A tram. A wildly rocking tram, overflowing, and more jumping on. The last purple and orange streaks above the central volcano, Misti. The clang of bells, the women in black. The gradual ebb away from the centre.

We gathered speed and night settled. Out through the perfect pattern of streets to a highway, the river, factories, slums, and then a racing mile or two through a temperate green valley. White volcanic stone glistened. Chacras, the little fields, waved with maize and the cloverlike alfalfa. Trucks loomed stationary in our path; we swerved, and nearly went into some donkeys trotting homewards through the dark. My host explained: we were filling in time until he could take me to meet his father. We had in fact to return to the city. His gloved hands gripped the wheel, the night constellations swung above us; he was a whole-hearted, a

demon driver. His driving struck an extreme of pride, the more
dangerous as he was all but fifty. He launched us back towards
Arequipa. Then it came out: it was his father's car. A nice weakness to have discovered in him.

Through the city again to the patrician quarter. We stopped
beside a high wall. There was an emblazoned gate then a small
patio, then a doorway tall as those of Zanzibar, a fine embossed
Arab doorway, opening on to the main patio, the sides made of
several rooms, beyond which was a third patio, again small, of
which I only caught a glimpse. Although the inspiration might be
Moorish, with origins even older still, the simple treatment, the
wealth of plants, the juxtaposition of indoors and out would certainly have appealed to a Japanese. There was an atmosphere of
rest and seclusion. But then, when we entered a living room, to
meet the Señora's mother and father, the objects that fitted this
first impression—old harmless pieces of furniture, sporting guns,
antique china—had all been pushed to the farther end, they were
there literally with backs to the wall, while near to in the used
area, the centre of stage near the fireplace, had been imported
a most garish three-piece suite of not very good bucket design,
and a long low table cum radiogram that though silent sang of its
unhappy colour. The whole thing jazzed. But they had obviously
chosen it.

They were a grave old couple, very dignified, straight as one of
the rejected chairs. He was dignified and sad, remote with a soft
sizzling of pride; he thought before speaking, he didn't hear well.
She was dignified and fretful, quick and decided point by point.
Their welcome was guarded. I came from their daughter.

But we didn't talk of that, except by reference to my acquaintance with all their family in Lima—a place as they named it that
receded and diminished. Indeed the father did say before I left
that in the old days, sailing to Europe, from their port of Mollendo
and then passing by Callao, that there they had never thought of
getting off to spend the transit hours in Lima. Arequipa families
stayed aboard. What should they have got off to see?

Coming myself from a Yorkshire family that views London

with some suspicion I took his point. Avoid contamination.

He tackled me actually on my being British. The British though they had assisted in the development of Peru had done even better for the enemy, Chile. It all went back to the Chilean War. Yes, that was eighty years ago but Peru had been ruined; there had been misery, bandits, exploitation, the growth of Lima. Why hadn't we built them better ships? "You sold us the *Huascar*, built at Birkenhead. There were thirty Englishmen in the crew. But you sold the Chileans the *Almirante Cochrane*, built at Hull, of three times the tonnage! We had Armstrong three-hundred pounders; they had Armstrong twelve tonners! They had officers with names like Cox, Edwards, Macpherson, Rogers, Walker, Wood! Señor, in the recent Spanish Civil War, the great Powers each tested their weapons. But in the Chilean War there was only Britain, pitting its ironclads one against the other. As in football, Hull against Birkenhead!" He twinkled gravely, then receded visibly. He asserted, "It was not without honour in the fight. As with your Drake, our Admiral Grau harried the enemy down the main. And on land our Colonel Caceres continued after other Peruvians had surrendered. Arequipa was besieged. The Chileans mounted their attack from the Peruvian capital . . . Lima." His ideas trailed off.

Señor Augusto commented, "My father is a student of the War of the Pacific. He is also a great friend of Britain. He approved of my sending George to study there."

The parents stared. This was a family matter.

The mother said, "We are a home-loving people. We stay close to the hogar, the hearth, Señor." She implied, "except for my erring daughter". "Only the air here makes us a bit nervous." There was a pause. No one had anything to say. "We love our houses and gardens," she continued. "At one time there was much visiting among families. My cousins . . ." but then she checked herself, perhaps seeing the danger of launching into names. The break was saved by someone else entering. This was her other daughter, Pilar.

I had heard of Pilar from Roberto, who, close on every subject but women, had uninvited given his opinion of her. For him she was a particular species of virgin, in the grip of the Church and a lifelong envy of his own mother Carmen Maria. So I was surprised to find her at once sympathetic, sheltered yes and by now angular, lean and shy and without presence, but tender of expression with dark round eyes that glowed with the quiet fires of passion. She had a soothing voice that evoked summer evenings, then sudden harsh catches in it. Her mouth though firm seemed to tremble secretly; she had black hair, a romantic face. It came out that she had just been to Mass.

She had no conversation either; so I looked at Augusto to see if we should leave. They wanted us to go, but somehow they were keeping us. I was tempted in blunt Yorkshire style to start talking about Juanita's pregnancy, or Roberto's studies, or Carmela's job, but clearly I had no right to do so. The Señora was assuredly there in that room behind every flicker of an eyelid, but it could not be said by any stranger, and stranger I rightly was to them. I suddenly thought I saw her sitting at the far end among the things of the past.

Pilar was saying something about Melgar—oh, had I heard of their poet, Melgar, who expressed the soul of Arequipa? She was eyeing me with covert curiosity, which to me said she knew I was a writer living in her sister's house in Lima (which meant, of course, they had all read the letter) and perhaps I could convey to her what it was like, could satisfy some of her fantastic curiosity to know about erring Carmen Maria. I said I had never heard of Melgar. I found these unspoken exchanges wearing. I asked in return if she played the piano; there was one halfway down the room.

To my surprise, at Augusto's bidding, she obliged. She was an accomplished performer and this obviously gave them great pleasure and satisfaction. Evenings with this sad gentle woman playing! The melancholy of it was heart-catching, the languor, the plaintiveness of a despedida, an old Moorish song of farewell, a sonnet of Melgar set to music, a piece of Chopin to show she could do it. She was telling about her own life, about a vanished epoch of the town.

The feeling of our encounter was transformed. Well... enough, as we left, for the mother to say, asking me if I knew America, that she had a grandson who was a doctor there. Nothing more, but she had referred to José, till now the Señora's most distinguished child. An odd, and calculated, insertion: a titbit to take back to Lima. Pilar's eyes glowed secretively.

No mention of course of my journey to Puno.

Señor Augusto now took me to the Club, a discreet oak-panelled establishment, where we were served with an excellent dinner. Shrimp soup hotly flavoured, a white fish, a delicate wine, roast pork with a heavier wine, crêpes suzette, coffee and liqueurs. I dare say, this falls flat, if the reader is not hungry, but for the writer at that moment it was a welcome repast (one could always, for the altitude, take sleeping pills) and gratifying to see my host so expanding, obviously now in a favourite posture, that the floodgates of confidence began to open. Lima, of course, his father was old-fashioned: people of ambition gravitated there. He himself had shares in companies. But he loved this region too much to desert it. He loved the late summer nights in the vineyards, the crystalline skies, the leisurely company. He was used to the fishing and duck shooting up on the puna; he liked the Indians.

I was surprised to hear this, but he repeated with a flourish that for the natural Indian, the aboriginal, he had, besides pity of course, admiration. He knew old men, heads of communities, whose memories were books the pages of which they could read off like learned monks. They could recite what their great-grandfathers had known. In their own environment, in the routine of farming, they had all the sagacity of countrymen. They were law-abiding, frugal, conscientious; they aimed for moderation and balance out of very ancient intuitions, oh long before the Incas, concerning man's destiny. They had reverence. Had I seen Indians kneeling in church? The Indian had a Christian soul. He was open to redemption.

Speaking, my host had warmed to his subject, most of all when he brought the Church into it, and after a good sip of wine he underlined this—"The Church is the key to the Indian remaining himself. Other forces threaten, of modern materialism. But the Church will not forsake its mission. My good Señor, God wills this work."

I then asked him if he knew any priests or missionaries working in the Puno area, as I was continuing there and would like to see something of the day-to-day life of the Indian. It was then he mentioned the Maryknoll Fathers and made me feel I must look them up. He had become graver, though; I was continuing to Puno? There was a question he was on the point of putting. We had more wine. I put one to him: hadn't his family haciendas in the area ... would it be possible for me to visit them?

My dear Señor ... there was nothing he wouldn't do for me. Unfortunately their own hacienda had been sold. One of his cousins still had a hacienda, actually it stretched half the way to Cuzco, but an American had visited it and then published a report, a most distorted and ignorant piece of journalism, and now the steward wouldn't let a stranger near. And his wife's family, their hacienda, there would be difficulties over that too. Only sheep and alpaca ranching, however; I could see it from the train. Pastoral existence.

"What did the American say?"

"Good Señor, he was a troublemaker. Some cholo had been talking to him. Because, do you see, the politicians here have taken up Agrarian Reform, every idiot now thinks himself an expert. Break up the estates, don't pay the owners—but what then happens to the economy? Cross the border into Bolivia and note the anarchy created there: or rather, how what was once the landowner's, the landowner who is a gentleman like me, has passed to the hands of the cholo middleman, who exploits the peasant as never before. I do not like the cholo, Señor. He degrades the simple Indian."

"Moreover," he brushed on, "if we need reform, it is not so much the latifundia, the large holding, but the minifundia, the peasant's strip, that needs rationalisation. That is, if we are to be scientific, efficient, up-to-the-minute, Señor!" He challenged me with sudden haughtiness. I too, as a writer, could go to the Devil: twice, for that matter, if I sided with his sister and her unspeakable miscegenation. But decorum at once softened it—"My plea is for time, consideration for traditions that once broken cannot return. The Indian is a unique repository of man's ancient wisdom concerning life. Your scientists should think of that."

We paused for coffee and liqueurs. He had made himself plain about the Echarris: simpler for him than asking directly if I was going to visit them.

But now impulsively, the romantic in him, the paradox in Latin nature, he wanted to speak about his sister and ask how she was getting on. He intimated that for all their reserve his parents equally were interested; if I stayed a few days they would ask me openly. After all, they had only met me that evening.

His walls, however, at this point were down. So I told him every good thing I could. What an unusually sweet woman was Juanita. (They had heard of the baby and he put it like this, that at least they would write as soon as it was born.) Of Carmela's pranks. How Roberto needed an older man of the family to guide him. And lastly about the good Señora, good devoted woman that she was. For me, who was not a Catholic, she seemed the epitome of all the virtues.

Coffee and liqueurs were down by now and possibly the furnace of digestion added to the warmth with which I pleaded. But in fact pleas were no longer called for; his furnace was roaring too, and a suppressed reality of devotion to his sister, and a sort of sporting tolerance of another kind of creature. She had made her life; in a hundred years the family would get the thing in proportion. God, he knew, watched over her.

As for Roberto, he noted what I said; indeed, this was his own impression; he would write on the matter to his cousin Carlos. He himself would be in Lima soon and as always would be calling on his sister.

So he called on her. Who would have guessed it?

"How often do you get up to Lima?"

"Oh ... once in two years. Sometimes three. You can remember me, my good Señor, as someone who does not run with the times. I am a countryman. A countryman."

And on this note his reserve returned, and a dreaming self-satisfaction. Rather stiffly he saw me to my hotel.

Next day he arranged a complete timetable: a student to take me to the university, himself to cocktails with a well-known family inhabiting a house every travel writer mentions, his second son to motor me about until it was time to go and dine with an English resident who was kindness itself: an overflowing of attention, courtesy, and regret that anyone should want to move on. That's how I remember Arequipa. His final patrician salute at the station, part flush of pride, part sad bemusement.

Arequipa, at seven thousand feet, was already in the mountains —in the folds of the western cordillera. The climb from here was to the high plateau, broadening towards Lake Titicaca and south-wards to the heart of Bolivia, while again to the east were further ridges, parapets above the jungle. It was a skyhigh world, as in Turkey or Tibet, called variously puna or altiplano, with the sierra, the more mountainous parts, all about; and I awoke next morning in the game little train to an impression of a billiard table among clouds, these glisteningly white, thick as coral, with depths of blue sky between. The light was metallically intense: one saw a river, a wide straggling course, or an expanse of puna with its threadbare scrub, tufts and cushions of ichu grass and moss-packed yareta bushes, with occasional gnarled twisted trees, and at a hundred yards one could select the details of a rock and its forms, or a man's face. Near to the rivers there was cultivation, away to the last possible stony patch, and beyond this herding country. There were flashes of colour in the sombre brown and the dark porphyritic rock, ferns and clover and, in the swamps, rushes, and there especially there were plovers and curlew. A heron disregarded our passage. But the chief creatures, who gave immediate beauty, beauty and pathos to this electric landscape were men and women and their tranquil herds.

My own gaze went to the herds—not only familiar sheep and cattle, but llamas, the most graceful beasts imaginable, and after them the silky vicuña and the black, or white, or mottled alpaca. This was a region that principally supplied my own native town of Bradford. What would a Bradford wool man make of this gaunt biblical scene? He would be caught up in it, beyond price and quality, by its intensified almost eerie presentation of a different order of time and place, as if, across light years, this was the moon.

With the herds were the people, a man on horseback or a boy or women squatting and spinning, and on the irrigated patches were little groups of workers, hoeing or ploughing or walking single file to the next piece of work to be done, or standing, preparing a chew of coca; and these, though a long way off, seemed near. And among them, or striding to the horizon, across this infinity of visible land, were the wanderers, passing by hut and settlement, silent and dogged as if for ever committed to a treadmill of unconquerable distance. The air, with the carriage window down, was thin; to some extent one's eyesight floated. This was life over twelve thousand feet.

At last, midmorning, we reached Puno. We came bustling round the verge of Lake Titicaca, past the reed dwellers and the translucent blue myth-gathering waters. In the port stood three British steamers, for the lake crossing to Guaqui in Bolivia, a startling link in the railway system; for as my guide book told me the earliest of these had been brought up nearly a century ago piece by piece on mules from the coast. I later met a travelling Inspector on one of these craft while I was looking over it. He was on deck staring down at the engines, at local men refitting some part, with the visionary splendour of the lake around him, muttering, "Oh Christ, another balls up!" But later as she sailed, on time, into the crimson glory of the sunset, she seemed to fit the legendary setting, to be equally the work of the god Viracocha, sailing now to the halls of the Incas. Poetry after all depended on men who were practical with spanners.

Into the station, and a rush of children overseered by a bully boy; and so to the hotel. The air was raw. There was a llama stepping down the street. It was like Brontë country in the matter of bleakness, a great deal more so, yet against the grey, the flinty walls and worn cobbles, the dun and the beige and the off-white, there was the interest of stately barred windows, baroque copings, romanesque towers. Tradition had consciously been at work. And the whole town rippled with colour, flashes and twitches of orange to purple in the passage of the many-skirted women. These were Aymara Indians, mostly cholas but some of humbler standing, a pocket of whom lived round Titicaca, a small cousinship of the greater population centred around La Paz in Bolivia; and visually their most distinctive feature, besides the flashing bell-shaped skirts, were their brown and black and grey bowlers, but mostly brown, perched slightly at an angle, on top of their plaited black hair. Their men by contrast were soberly clad, for the most part in dark European garb, an occasional drover or road worker wearing a wool bonnet with ear flaps, but then with a squashed trilby on top. Ponchos, in town, were not in evidence.

Puno was also the market centre for a large Quechua population; though, I was told, except among cholos, there was not much marriage with the isolationist Aymaras, and also details of dress were distinct. But all this was beginning to blur, through new appetites, and the effect of schooling; and then there was such a thing as fashion—walking through the weekend market I couldn't see a peasant without her bowler.

I mention this because I had learned in Lima, from Juanita just before leaving, that the Echarris by now were pretty mongrel—Spanish only through a Basque captain who had roistered in seventeenth Potosí, blithely spending his cut from a mine. The woman whose children had taken his name had never been formally married to him; little was remembered, but she had been Quechua, of some rank and of great beauty, and after his death she had been sought by others. Her children had not fared too well. A century later they had lost half their land, and the rest of it at the start of the Republic: one encroachment after another ceding it to the Montellano ranches; and they themselves had fallen into serfdom. But then some ancient vitality had stirred: generation by generation they had inched back up the ladder, through strength of character getting the posts that carried weight in their peasant community—the church jobs, the fiesta steward-ships—finally to become the Montellano mayordomos. It was this far that Juan had reached, Juanita's great-grandfather; and Juan had married an Aymara chola. From this union José had come, most dynamic figure of them all, who had stopped at nothing to break his chains and make his fortune and buy back the land that he believed belonged to him. Juanita had not been more specific, but it was easy to guess who had done the selling, who, declining in wealth, had had to do it. At the same time, roughly, his son the Doctor had won a Montellano for a wife.

It was said of José that he could have gambled with the Devil and have been the one to show a straight flush.

He had died two years before.

It was now his other and older son, Silvestre, present head of the Echarris, to whom I was bearing a letter from the Señora, and a gift of imported caviar, and some fine cigars and a bottle of whisky. She had told me I would like him, the patrón as he was called, rough diamond though he might seem to be. I had had no difficulty in finding his house, adjunct to his transport yard; though from the other side it looked like a battered rambling farm-house leaning up behind the high street wall.

Nobody seemed to be at home; then a woman appeared, but she didn't understand me. There was another woman, they both looked Quechua, the rounded rather than the eagle face, and children edged into view to stare; and then a very old woman in black skirts came casting spells—or so it seemed: which done, she informed me that the patrón was away. Where? Hmm, in his transport yard. He was not in his yard. Hmm, in the fields. The fields? Or, hmm, he could be in Juliaca, La Paz, Lima . . . her tongue slyly wagged. Then she croaked a laugh. It was a negative welcome.

I went back to the transport yard, and a similar rigmarole took place. It was as if they needed to know why I wanted him, and how I, an obvious tourist gringo, could be fitted into life as they knew it, before they could remember where he was. It was as if to shield him from bad luck. Would he be there later? Nobody knew.

Then a car pulled in, and a man with sharp lightly burnished features and a damaged eye came over. He listened to me, mused for a time, and said, "The patrón will be glad to see you. You bring him news? He will be glad to see you. But for the moment . . . he must be very busy. He has" . . . he felt he must offer me something . . . "much new land to think about."

As I looked blank he continued, "The rains! All are out in the fields, sowing. Without the rains, no one could live. You must speak to the patrón, as soon as he is here." He was about to leave me, then thought further. "You are at the hotel? I will call to tell you."

So I went away and wandered about and looked up the Mary-knoll Fathers.

Next morning at some unearthly hour, the dawn dripping into the garden, a hotel boy knocked to tell me that there was a man below with the car for Juliaca. I knew nothing about it, and he went away. He returned to say that the man expected me, and it was also the car that went to Pomata. Had I ordered it for Pomata? I now got up, got dressed, swore; though as Pomato, I had read, was a place to visit, why not profit from this odd opportunity? I yelled at the boy to get me some breakfast, and lunged downstairs to question the driver.

It was my contact of the day before.

Politely he murmured, "Buenos dias, Señor."

I must admit, apart from the hotel, snoring still in velvet somnolence, four-thirty found the rest of the town pullulating with activity. The sky was awake and so were the people, dodging like mice, very bright little mice in their best rig-out, from store to store, laying out the market scene or boarding buses or striking out on foot for a change of markets on this occasion. The fishers were coming in from the lake. Church custodians had opened their doors. Within seconds it seemed perfectly normal.

The man explained that he was a chauffeur, the driver of an Echarri "expreso" plying usually between Puno and Juliaca, though on Sundays he did do trips along the Lake as far as Copacabana and its pilgrim shrine. He was also of course one of the family, a cousin (I learned later, an Aymara cousin), and he brought me a message from the patrón.

So he was not going to Pomato? Oh no, he had people today for Juliaca. He must be off, to collect them, house by house; he was late. But he would be back by afternoon, and it was then also the patrón expected me.

Afternoon? Then why in the world. . . ?

"Bueno, Señor!" He had felt it right to warn me.

Third time lucky, one could but hope, but when that afternoon I returned to the house the patrón was not there yet. It had filled up, however, with people, and the chicha was finding its way about. More geniality prevailed; the old woman stood over me and smiled, though when she thought I wasn't looking I caught her eyes searching my soul. The other women suddenly spoke Spanish, though words only and without conviction; one of their children tried me with English. The time passed, though, because abruptly there was a quarrel, in an antechamber of this principal room, a screaming man and woman affair, in Quechua but its tone was universal. The man's voice was gruff and complaining, the woman's inevitably found other arguments: hammer and tongs, daring each other, and then with a yell she had run away. Heightened discussion among everyone present, then the sound of him tramping out to the street. At this point Justo, my contact, appeared.

Señor Justo. Well, I was glad to see him: one step nearer, I felt, to the patrón. He dismissed my curiosity about the quarrel. Chicha drinking, something on their mind; but in general this didn't happen in the family. Yes, everyone in the house was a relative: who else should they invite here? Yes, he conceded, it sometimes happened even among the quietest couples that a shirt wasn't clean or the money was short, that she could be jealous or he could be drunk: but the compadres regulated everything. No one went to the prefectura. Everything worked for order and harmony.

He spoke carefully, restraining himself, but his voice went on, telling me more; with a sort of dark smile he was spilling the beans—how sometimes it happened the other way round, that it was not the man who beat the woman but she who took a stick to him. It depended on who overstepped the line, the line clearly drawn between spheres. Which of them offended custom. Custom was the regulating factor. In a big family—

The patrón had entered. Silvestre Echarri. One knew him at a glance. Justo backed into silence and sharp watchfulness. The room readjusted, the news of arrival echoed through the surrounding porches, and from this point on in order of importance the family gathered in respectful nearness, which left most of them however in outer rooms. Echarri was a man of about sixty, short with an immense bull chest, a shock of hair, fleshy mouth and eyes, and a look of power and stubbornness about him. He seemed to pause, till all were in position, everything down to some grand-daughter's pin, then he exploded with a gargantuan greeting. He smiled, one could just call it a smile, he did not attempt a coastal abrazzo, but he extended to his immense uttermost and proclaimed welcome. Chicha for everyone!

Then, as soon as he had absorbed me and the gifts, he proclaimed what was really the cause for rejoicing. He had heard by phone from his brother's widow, yes, the same, the complete man they had loved: that her daughter Juanita, yes, the one who had married into a Huancayo family, but now they lived in Lima, had had a daughter. Yes, only a daughter. But he would go to the baptism. For they had asked him to be godfather.

The letter I brought made the same propostion. He was a very satisfied man at this minute.

He led the drinking, he was a born leader, a cheer leader with a

decorated gourd that was filled and emptied ceremoniously—
not quite the style of a kava ceremony but the Andean emphasis
was placed on quantity; he had a keen eye for the level of my
tumbler, and, worse, when bottles of spirit appeared, he set a
glass of spirit beside me, challenged, and downed his own at a
swallow. Out of an ordinary Sunday afternoon another of these
frightful orgies was starting. But I was wrong: for him these were
casual drinks, that made him wax conversational. "Señor Sykes,"
he took great trouble with the name, "what do you drink in
England? You come from England? That is a long way. Could I
send a son to school there?" He gave his dry thick smile dis-
counting the question. "I understand that education is important.
I had to do without it myself. My brother had it, though."

At mention of his brother, all those near made respectful noises;
a woman exclaimed, "he is dead, dead!" and burst into sobs. There
was clucking of tongues. The patrón reminded them what a
good man had lived, and how he himself, who had attended the
funeral, had eaten the last supper by the body and had helped to
bear the bier to the grave. The procession had halted outside the
hospital to hear speeches from learned men. "You were not
there but I describe it to you!" He pumped respect and reverence
into them.

A confused medley of response followed, much of it in
Quechua; and a woman's voice repeated some words with such
insistence that I asked Justo for their meaning. "She says she has
seen the Doctor dancing behind a mask in one of our fiestas!
I do not think so. Some believe it. With chicha in them . . ." He
edged back as the patrón's eye swung round.

"Justo!"

"Patrón."

"You remember last year? How your family found their fields
had been robbed? Has there been any such trouble again, or hint
or talk of robbers in the valley? Have you watched well?"

"Sí, patrón. My brothers have watched, and it was not a hard
winter. The poor steal when they have to eat."

"They steal because you are also my family. Men begin to

steal from me. It has happened today in another district." The patrón drummed attention to his words, to his sole point of view and authority. He was giving Justo a pretty hard look. He switched to me, "There is theft in England? It is the same trouble the world over; men grow envious of one another. But no one dared to steal from my father!" His look was such that I too would soon have been questioning my integrity; but he touched my arm, "Salud, Señor!" He turned to speak to his other side.

More of the family were filtering in, respectfully, with an eye on the chief, but among themselves livening up. The women in traditional dress were jolliest, serving the chicha, clearing space to the table that apart from the chairs we were sitting on, a radio set, a wall-high dresser, was almost the only furniture. The young people, a few of them, looked ready for a chorus from "Oklahoma", but the main note was drab agricultural—this could have been a country committee room or public bar with something special afoot: though later it took on a fiercer air as if swamped by a revolutionary mêlée. Even now sheer vigour edged towards explosion. This group was a confident hard force. It could feel its strength; perhaps not its direction. The patrón so far supplied that.

Which of them was the patrón's wife? That was impossible to say. The introduction was not made. On his other side sat compadres; and when he spoke to the women, he spoke in Quechua. His own Spanish was perfectly good, but on balance it was not the main tongue here. Perhaps Aymara was spoken also, I do not know; apart from Justo, the Aymara features, the lighter narrower dourer face, were not conspicuously present. The Aymara side of the family probably centred round another household.

The old woman had crept up to us. She had been near enough to hear the exchange between Justo and the patrón, and she had since been muttering to herself.

"What is it, old one?" he suddenly called to her. "Have you news for me? Will all be well?" He was at the same moment refilling my glass, the glass for the local slightly watered spirit, so he spoke to her in Spanish. He said to me, "She is bringing me news about the baptism!"

But crankily she kept on muttering, then said, "You should pray to the saints, patrón. If men steal, they are angry with you, they could do worse things to you. Seek counsel concerning the new land."

He glared. "I did not ask you about those questions." He said something to her in Quechua. She smiled and was leaving, but he called her back. "Come, Tia, have you asked the coca? You have your wisdom. Give it to me."

She returned and shot out something in Quechua.

He did not look at all pleased.

I learned later from Justo what she had said: that it was good to be a godfather, but not to mount ambition on it. The explanation: the patrón might use a visit to Lima to expand commercially. He had some such plans for his son, Julio. The moment, the baptism, would be most auspicious. But the old woman strongly disapproved, she disapproved of them leaving their ancestral territory —she had made an exception, eventually, of the Doctor—and usually the patrón listened to her. She was his aunt, José's remaining sister; she had always been religious and in her old age she had learned other traditional secrets, that helped her to foresee the future. The younger women were uneasy with her.

The patrón, however, regained his humour the minute she had left us. The drinking was affecting him at last. Steaming food was coming to the table, where there was room for eight of us, the others eating in the passageway round the courtyard or in the kitchen. With punctilio we took out places and our bowls were passed up for shacuy, a creamy bean soup with herbs. We were served by a gaunt majestic woman who could have been the patrón's wife, she was addressed as Mame, or Mamai, and there was a set honorific phraseology as each received his bowl of soup. Then, there was a crescendo of eating noises, a unison of tribute and thanks, a counterpointing of scraping noises, a timely belch, and we were ready for more, which the patrón saw that we all had. There was bread by each of us, fresh Sunday bread; one mentions this because I was soon to learn that bread was a luxury up on the puna; as also I learned that the only meat seemed to be this tough dried meat, from which animal I can't imagine, that on this occasion appeared next with the hash, potato inevitably, with bitter beans, and green squash, and pepper seasoning. There were communal dishes of powdery grains, but I left those well alone. I can't pretend I enjoyed the meal, except for the soup and then second-hand through others' enjoyment: the trouble for me was not in the tastes, very tasty, but in the look of things. I suddenly felt unadventurous, although I had sampled most of it before. I would have given anything for fish and chips—at that moment I understood my countrymen who braving the world in coach tours ask everywhere for tea and toast. Perhaps, cumulatively, it was the smell of the room. It was a cold afternoon, after a burst of rain, and the heat was provided by this mass of bodies. The only solution was to down more alcohol.

This of course was generously provided. Drinking did not stop for the food. The patrón led, and he was becoming voluble—about his father, the great José. It was the thought of the thieving that rankled, and how none would have dared it against his father —if they had, crack! He would have taken a whip to them, or a length of rope, or his bare hand. Why, his father had burned down people's houses, and set his family on to stone them. No one had persisted in opposing his father.

The result: he had built the transport company, and recovered nearly all their lands.

"Am I not right to continue in his footsteps?" The patrón looked about him, glowering. It was a boast, an appeal for support, an admission that finally he was but the son. He was calling on them in José's name.

There were grunts and murmurs of solidarity.

"We will work the new fields," he said.

He proclaimed to me, "All work in our family. We are a team; each has his job; and this continues throughout the year. We follow the seasons. At this time, we sow. But the good time is after the rain; you should have come to see us in May."

"May I go out to the fields to watch?"

He laughed. "Watch?" He instructed Justo. He said, still smiling, amused at this gringo who had come across the seas to watch, "Perhaps you will spot the thieves for us!" He clapped me on the shoulder. There were good-natured guffaws. Everyone had a swig of chicha. We were ending the meal with a sweet corn pudding. He said, "We now sow more than we need, and with the surplus we buy more land. We sow that land, and with the surplus, again we buy more land; and then with that surplus, the accumulated surplus, we shall one day build a factory. This is the direction my father pointed. He owned a truck, then ten trucks, a bus, taxis—a transport company! We are strong people here. Not only here."

There were nods, sideways they were observing me. There had been no further mention of Lima, and nothing at all concerning Arequipa, but these well-to-do farmers so lately peasants, these thrusting ambitious entrepreneurs, knew that I must have heard about them, and without caring very much were adding, through the patrón, their own proud information. They were a sceptical keen ruthless company, disciplined only by his word, if one excepted the old woman's admonitions. They had got hold of this idea of capital, and it would obviously see them to the top of the tree.

Only their habits dragged a bit behind.

The inevitable next stage was arriving: fuddled loquacious humour, querulousness, incontinence, stupor.

It was difficult leaving. The patrón's geniality was quick to take offence. See the evening through, please, with him.

Justo got me out. He had a strange role there. The old woman lurked in the doorway.

I was never completely at ease with Justo, because I couldn't quite see where he stood. Perhaps his damaged eye was disconcerting, a relic of one of José's frays; and his other sharp almond eye was watchful in the manner of one who in turn is watched. He was pursuing a course of his own, one felt, within the family position assigned to him, and this made him wary. He could be critical in his roundabout way, his guarded yet finally garulous way, concerning the patrón's rule of the family—in part this was simply contrasting it with the father's, whose absolute trusty he had been; yet suddenly the most innocent question silenced him, or the most innocent request to see this or that met with an incontrovertible no. It was as if I might turn some procedure against him. He had to put up a quota of refusals. Then, unexpectedly, he would spill more beans. Through him I got the feel of the rasp rubbing within the family bosom.

Over the next week I saw him often. He ran me to certain selected fields; I did journeys with him north to Juliaca and south by the Lake side to Pomata. It was wonderful just to be moving about in this vast crystal ball of a world, glittering with changes of light, swinging new mirages into view, so that an intense actinic sky over here gave, over there, before a purple storm arrowing down at the entrance to a valley and again over there in the centre of the Lake, with golden space swimming between. A storm would circle us, beat black murder, would dissolve in mist: then that too would go leaving puffed white clouds and a rinsed heaven and a somehow differently arranged landscape. Illimani, Sorata, Ancohuma, Condoriri, the snow-capped giants, had shifted closed. Ripples of wind chilled the lake and chased after shadows across the plain.

The fields we visited were in the lee of hills and watered by a stream. The dry season potato was out and the best land was going to quinoa and oca and several varieties of potato, some to come up quicker than others; with a sowing of beans and barley in the hollows, the later for animal fodder in May. May, it was repeated, was the great month, the heart of their autumnal harvesting, with cutting of quinoa and digging of potatoes and a high-tide of fiestas. Now was the lean time of the year, hard work and not much to eat.

The working procedure, after breakfast at six of herb tea, toasted grain, soup, was for the men to plough the fields into furrows, using the primitive Egyptian plough introduced by the

Spanish, with a long wooden shaft and iron blade and drawn by a
yoke of oxen; and for the women and children to sow and plant
and hoe the soil over. The area was dotted with tiny groups of
people, some of them working their own land, some working
land they had had to sell to the patrón, some working land he had
bought with them on it—so that in fact he employed peons,
"colonos", just as once the Montellanos had employed him—
and some of it worked by extra hands called in for a wage of
coca and potato. Young children brought the midday food,
skipped about, or attacked the soil with an ancient type of digging
stick; by twelve years of age they were working with their
mothers, at nineteen beside their fathers. The rhythm that at first
looked slow never in fact lost a minute; it was intense, dedicated,
astonishingly fast, and as if that entire panorama of figures were
linked antlike by a special sense that kept them moving forward
together. Women sometimes sang in unison, or bewailed the
stinging approach of rain. Rain or no, the work went on. The
men stopped only to prepare coca, and for the midday meal,
which might be a gruel or hash brought out to them in jars.

Justo remarked, "They are anxious this year. The prediction is
for floods and calamities. The ancient people have been disturbed."

"Ancient people?"

"The spirits of the fields. There have been too many changes
lately."

This was a hint, following on others, that the patrón's policy of
amassing land and turning its owners into a labour force that, like
other proprietors, he kept undernourished (for the land whose
use they got in payment, for their three to four days work per
week for him, was less than they had had before, and stonier) was
an offence against justice and tradition. These men needed more
land, not less. Aymaras, they were undyingly independent. The
patrón's father, the old man, would never have profiteered out
of hunger, or out of other difficulties, to buy up land, whatever
his methods in the realm of transport. These developments were
dividing the family.

"But aren't small strips uneconomic?" I was remembering

Augusto and his words on minifundia. "Isn't it sensible to con-
solidate them; and, well, yes, not work them like this . . . but as
a co-operative, a farming co-operative? As in the remaining free
communities . . . as in Inca times . . . or, as you may have heard,
what they have tried successfully in Vicos, to the north of Peru?"

"Or in Cuba!" Justo's teeth flashed, his face wreathed in dark
secretiveness.

"Do you hear about Cuba, Señor Justo? Your papers don't give
much idea."

"We hear." He sucked his teeth in "Every night in Puno you
can listen to Moscow Radio, in Quechua. If you want to." He
was abruptly very active with the car, as if it were a difficult
steed. His expression set. No more questions.

I asked, "And the other side of the family, the Quechua cousins,
is their land being capitalised, like this?"

No answer.

I hurried on, "I thought the patrón said it was grazing land
mostly. Sheep and alpaca and some vicuña. Drovers, shepherds.
Could we go and see that?"

After some persistence I prised out of him that such a visit was
not on the cards. He was warily enigmatic again. He glanced to
the sides, into his mirror. He found an occasion to praise the
patrón. His eye, the damaged one, seemed to hurt him. He offered
me a cigarette but then withdrew from conversation. Nothing to
do but drink in more landscape.

He spilled another small bean, however, when it was arranged
next day he should drop me off in Juli, a town midway down the
Lake, important once as a Jesuit centre and where I was to visit
some of the Maryknoll Fathers. It began by his sneering at the
missionaries. "But why?" For some minutes he was not com-
municative. Then slyly, having had time to think it out, he
ventured, "They disrupt our customs. They disturb the young
people. With us, if a boy wants a girl, he throws a stone at her or
a clod of earth; if she wants him they go behind a tree, or into a
ditch, or to a field hut. Or sometimes the parents have fixed it up.
But then, and so far there are no obligations—no chicha, no

presents of food exchanged—the girl comes to live in his family:
to make sure she is fertile and doesn't make trouble. They can
live a year, or more, together, free and easy, sorting it out. Then
in Lent we have 'la ronda'—the round-up: and some dozen or
more couples get spliced. Some dozen or more tied up each year.
It is not so expensive like that, either, for the cost of Mass and
feasting is shared."

"But the priests, I suppose, call it sinful?"

"Huh! With these new catechists of theirs! The result, some
youngsters now go to the church after only a month together.
That is more costly, and often too quick. What if the girl is not a
good one?" He spat swiftly out of the window. "We have always
paid too highly to the priests. I am a Catholic but I see they weigh
too heavily." He carried in fact a miniature crucifix and pictures
of the saints above the windscreen. "But we cannot do without
them," he concluded; "not today, though perhaps, tomorrow…"

"Hasn't Castro said that, Señor Justo?"

But Señor Justo was again fading out and appeared not to have
heard the question. He switched on the radio to highland music
and blew his horn to scatter some peasants cutting across the road
with their flocks. In the driver's seat he paid scant respect to these
slow earthbound comrades of his.

Yet a few minutes later as we left the part where the hills came
close in to the Lake, and the wide plain spun again before us,
luminous and speckled with figures, more tiny working groups
for miles ahead sowing their year's food supply, he said simply,
"We love our land; and we love our families. We demand only
enough to live decently in peace. That is not excessive, Señor.
But for the rest, I have no liking." And his face grew taut as
though seeing ahead to a day of very sharp knives.

He dropped me in Juli where I lunched with the Fathers.
Americans under their habits to a man, they asked me about the
Berlin situation. Why did Britain cavil so? What did we think of
President Kennedy? How was it over there in London?

The meal over we passed by the church, one of the exotic little
churches of Juli that bespoke early colonial fervour run riot in the

minds of mestizo carvers, the mysteries of the Church decorated with sly earthy humour. The padres made obeisance and cast practical eyes over the work of reconstruction. The rubble of indifference was being removed, the frescoes being repainted; the congregation was being regathered from all the countryside about; after at least a century of neglect, for with Spain's departure there had been a lack of priests, the Word was being cultured again. This time with American backing.

On the way out to a peasant community, in a solid-looking Ford truck Padre C. explained their task. The people, lacking priests, had lapsed in the Faith. To bring them back to the living church meant step by step indoctrination; and for this they had recruited lay brethren, "catequistas", who schooled and aided by a book of instruction held classes within their several family groups, bringing the Creed, Communion, the Bible into recognition again. District directors overseered the catechists, and these in turn worked close with the priest: so that one priest caring for a widespread parish (or possibly ten or fifteen parishes) now found as he laboured round his circuit that people, at least far more than formerly, were prepared for confession and the holding of Communion.

It was the system the early Jesuits had used, and as then there was a receptive flowering. These people really loved God, he affirmed.

Such was the framework, and within this framework, steadied here and there by a new pair of boots and always the small satisfactions of office, other advances were being made. You wanted people for vaccination or to hear the Agricultural Officer? Fine. Tell the catechist to gather them. You wanted to start them learning Spanish or to learn how to work a credit co-operative? Fine. The catechist would beat his iron bar, put out his flag, the people would gather. These Indians had seen they could trust the padres. Some time back, if they had needed a loan, they had been saddled with fifty per cent interest. Today, in their own credit co-operatives, put together mite by mite, there were average holdings of ninety dollars apiece, that had already supported loans to members of over one million dollars. From one member, there were now four thousand members, in this single Department of Puno; and from here the movement had spread throughout Peru, to bring in forty thousand families. Progress! Self-help! Stability! And . . . interest rate of only six per cent!

It was perhaps an allowable confusion, but listening to him I imagined I was listening to Benjamin Franklin. Padre A. and Padre B., that I had already met in Puno, and Padre D. whom I was to meet in Cuzco, were though tough more typical churchmen, the two former ecstatically overflowing with the wonders of the eucharist, their striding garments yawning with emotion, and the last, the one who had inspired this mission, a gaunt beatifically still visionary as if depicted by Piero della Francesca; but Padre C., big boned and slangy, handling the Ford like a reluctant steer, was a throughway for every good notion that the Western world had to impart.

"Hey there!" He'd wave some Indians. "Boy, I just love these people," he'd say, "they're so responsive! They need a little love; but don't we all?" He'd offer me a toffee. "Your heart okay at this altitude?" I admitted it was beginning to squeak. "You couldn't take it long. I can't take it long. I work all out, then I go on vacation; then I come back here and work all out. I can't work as hard as these Indians, though. Boy, they're a really beautiful people. All they ask for is a little love."

He swung the truck up a valley track. The afternoon sky had clouded over, pressing the light down close to the earth; it was a comparatively deserted valley, it had the clarity at this moment of an out-of-season beach waiting for figures to reappear—and here they came, two Aymara women, leaning forward a little as they walked as if up deck against a wind, sturdy fishwife sort of figures with babies slung in their shawls behind, struggling at a fast pace forward. Then a man, at the same gait, preoccupied. Then a building and people working near it.

"The rural school," the padre explained. "It comes into the Food for Peace programme. Our Mission does the distribution. Back home, you see, they have too much food; they overproduce basic food. But right here the little children are starving; till now they've been too hungry to learn."

He broke off crisply, to wave to the people. He brought the truck to a stylish stop. He cried "Hey!", then spoke in twangy Aymara—he turned to explain: "For a time these people couldn't believe I was speaking Aymara! They could hear it but they could not believe it. Someone else had to convince them. But they understand me."

Rapidly, as he spoke, he was moving about, blessing a mother with a sick child, blessing a straw basket of seed, inspecting a sizzling stewpot of soup watched over by a triumvirate of mothers. Inside the school the children, at attention, sang a song, then were praised and inspected for the new bloom appearing on their cheeks. Did they like the food? Good, carry on. His active robes skimmed through the building—repairs to be done, more clothing needed, more first alphabet books. Outside again, he waited for a man coming at a run across the fields. They conferred together; it was the local catechist. "Good," announced the padre; "next stop the village." The catechist clambered up behind. All the children waved as we departed.

The centre of this old Indian community, that had owned this land and three times as much way back before Inca times, was round a first turn in the hills, very bleak, a last stony refuge. There was a scatter of buildings closing to the centre about a rough earth square, a white-washed church, a clump of trees. Dogs barked, there were faces at the doors of the low-walled compounds within which were the huts, the pen for sheep and alpaca and cattle, and all the daily domesticity; but apart from a pack of llamas and a donkey loaded with brushwood and being driven ahead of us there was no activity outside the walls. We stopped by one of the central compounds. Led by the catechist we entered and I spied, first thing, a pail of urine gently fermenting in a corner; we rounded a hut and faced the porch of the central hut and came to the door there, it was a reed-thatched adobe hut without windows, and within it was dark and, as I later observed, it was empty of all except a few utensils, a large chest, some clothing hung up, a crucifix, and a low earthen ledge wide enough to sleep on. It was at best a shepherd's occasional hut, a campaigning sentry's one-night guard-house: but built and rebuilt every eighty years or so it had been inhabited by this family for centuries. And except in the very coldest weather they slept seemingly out on the porch, wrapped in their sheepskins, blankets, ponchos. Their level of physical provision was not much different from that of their animals.

But they were free, of course; they were free men. They owed their labour only to themselves—at most they were called upon to provide assistance in road building and other public works, La Republica or faena it was called, legally frowned on but in practice universal throughout the country districts, a cheap way from the authorities' point of view of getting the modern services established: but this was seasonable, and not too offensive: it still left them free, the vital point, to till their own land for themselves. They were not serfs. They were land-holding Indians. This was a free peasant community, a comunidad, similar to the ayllu of Inca times.

They were starving, more or less (the padre told me later: as the talk in the community was all in Aymara the explanations had to come later), they had been whittled out of their best land—well, sometimes, they themselves had sold it to pay for food after a bad harvest; they had sold fields to build the church, and to have more splendid fiestas; but in the main the lawyers had tricked them out of it, bigtime ranchers applying the pressure—and now, with a steady increase in number, the land was no longer enough to support them. Many had left to sell their labour (to become serfs on estates locked away near the jungle, or seasonal workers on the coastal haciendas, or a part of Lima's slum mob); the rest continued, winter and summer, eking out what the hard land gave. Right now, they were living on American charity. Once a week in the church grain was distributed.

The headman, and a group of his fellows, for all discussion and decision affecting the community was undertaken in counsel, met the padre and we sat on the porch, on a short earthen bench, and they squatted about us, the catechist standing in the background. They were more earthy and homespun and sad than the cholos, but by no means as wretched as the peons of Huancayo or the besotted poor in the alleys of Ayacucho. They were impoverished, but proud, stubborn, independent. One could feel, as Señor Augusto had said, that they had ancient country wisdom behind them. At the same time they clearly liked the padre and were spontaneously ready for his ideas.

Two women bobbed out from the next hut and offered their guests a small glass of spirit. They were magnificent eyed, unruly women, with a strong sour smell about them. Children followed, and were sent back, then the women too retired.

The discussion centred round the possibility of getting a loan from the credit co-operative, in which this community participated, for the purchase of a tractor to pull in more land. It was a tortuous discussion, for their credit was low, no one else was likely to back them except possibly the Agricultural Bank and there a higher interest rate was called for, and that was the path to dangerous indebtedness; and in any case, though half of them wanted a tractor, wanted to see its gleaming metal, the other half thought the land more profitable if left as now for grazing. So, the padre, the man of God, must advise them.

"So what did you say?" I asked as we left and he recounted the discussion.

"Well . . ." It had not been easy for him. He could have said "Do this, I say so"; but then, how could they claim to be free? Freedom necessitated choice. He had been sidetracked within his own mind: the sort of problem he'd been set in seminary. For not to advise them, or to moralise, might equally sap their powers of achievement. It was not so easy being a priest among such very poor people. He was not one who preached Christ alone.

"So?"

"So I said, you could rent a tractor! My catechist tells me of another community, better placed, that would be willing to lease one; and we, the office of the credit co-operative, would do all the guaranteeing. You could experiment with one, just to see. That way, not too much commitment."

"And?"

"Why, you saw . . . that surge of agreement! They reckoned the voice of Solomon had spoken. That's why I led them to the church, to get things into perspective."

It was true, the elders had stared at the padre making his everyday suggestion as if divine light shone there—it was the psychology perhaps of their desperate situation; and he had straightway marched them off to the church, the thumb-sized Andean church that was white without and dark within, a womb of softly burning candles that had brought the Indians directly to their knees lapped by that protective glow. As he saw it, that had put things into perspective. All had kneeled in reverent silence, the Indians gazing at the sweet Madonna, and at a tortured saint, and at the strength of Jesus, and then, as if themselves pierced by the agony and the unfathomable mystery of this story, yet one so akin to their personal sorrow, they had bowed low, deep into the earth, their faces tearful, their bodies humbled. A silent candle-lit abasement.

"Well, it's not easy," concluded the padre. "But give us time, we'll save these people. We'll revolutionise the highlands."

"Will the politicians let you?"

"The Communists won't, but we're fighting the Communists. Our catechists stall any meeting where a Communist aims to speak. The big ranchers don't like us either. They have been suppressing our catechists; they're afraid when their peasants congregate even for bible study. They fear a Syndicato'll get formed. Mestizo landlords are nearly as difficult."

"Have you run across the Echarri family?"

He smiled ruefully. "I sure have. My first assignment here on the puna was to tackle old José Echarri. He died before I could win him over. But the people trust us. We shall win through the people."

"You seem to be distrusted by both extremes."

"The middle way generally is. I don't just say it is God's way—

for He can be extreme when He chooses; but here right now what other way can bring these illiterate rejected people, without bloodshed, into the nation?"

"Land Reform? Mass education? Effective local government? Co-operative trading?"

"Okay; though it'll need American money. But even so, how'll it work if the peasant can't read, can't vote, isn't ready? We say prepare him too, and do it through love and Christian brotherhood so that his guiding intelligence remains of the Spirit. Inside the man, inside what makes him tick. Not all to come packaged from Lima!"

"I can see, Padre, it's not easy," I agreed with him.

"Is it easy over there in England? Has Europe solved its every little problem? Have we in the States? Would it be healthy if we had?"

Jauntily, overbrimming with libido, the good padre swung the truck back to Juli. We had coffee and delicious Southern pie. Then he fixed me a lift back to Puno. He gave a brisk wave from the market place.

Next morning, Saturday, Justo appeared eyeing me as if I had myself taken orders. He sniffed as if sniffing a priestly smell. He was bearing an invitation from the patrón, to make my final weekend eventful, for the coming Tuesday I was continuing to Cuzco; but he loitered over it, seeking provocation. He needed in some way to smear the missionaries, Americans to boot, an outsize target; but caution and possibly inbred fear towards anything holy held him silent; he had first to be provoked. I was disinclined to do it. He eyed me with a growing disappointment . . . all gringos stuck together. . . .

So he had provoked me! I was smiling, half-vexed, rising despite good sense to the bait. I didn't like the look that said You Gringos! I remarked, "I can see you don't like the Padres, if they set up co-operative schemes that rival Echarri 'capitalist' interests!" I said this mouthful very softly, implying it was not too serious.

Even more softly came the answer, "Oh no, Señor, there you are wrong. If now there is more credit about, we can sell more kerosene and more fertilisers. As 'capitalists' we have a stake in that trade. We can charge more fares in our buses. If those comuneros become stronger, good! We like people with money to give us."

"Señor Justo, whose voice are you speaking with?" His old campaigner's face darkening, he looked abruptly very serious, his ideals, his sectarian politics gone, defence of the family (to the death) in their place.

"My voice, Señor. The voice of a Puneño." He was still aggressive. It was an absurd moment. We had quarrelled in a flash out of nothing; though, equally, it had to be put right at once. How? I was not prepared to betray the good Padres, drop in the ocean though their work might be when set against the stark shortage of time. I said, improvising, "Señor Justo, please tell the patrón that I cannot come tomorrow." A few minutes before I had accepted the invitation.

He reddened. "Señor, I cannot say that." No more he could, for because of Lima the patrón would come to see why for himself. This might not go well for Justo. He added, improvising in turn, "I think we misunderstood each other. What we have just spoke of is . . . nothing."

"I had much rather we spoke of Fidel Castro. Could you take me to one of your meetings?"

Meetings? He seemed not to have heard. But as quickly we were back where we usually were, he enigmatic, perhaps enjoying the role, I the visitor to be suitably impressed with the terrible things about to happen, in so far as hints could convey them. His flush had gone. He looked even a shade pleased to discover that there was metal in a gringo. Our relationship had been improved.

I was taken to a meeting—by the patrón himself; though needless to say it was not Fidelista. It was a Sunday afternoon cockfight. It was a nasty experience of flying feathers and blood, that out of respect I had to sit through. These country folk revelled in it. The birds had been trained for a month past, trimmed and rubbed down and rationed, and for the last days kept in the dark, super-ready, like commandos, to kill. They were carried into the pit by their owners, all quite well-to-do cholos, coloured cloths over the birds' heads. The cloths were removed, the birds held to within pecking distance of each other, for a preliminary bite and scratch that sent a first feather fluttering down; then they were taken aside to be spurred.

Now followed almost an interval, a most leisurely time to make your bet. Around the pit were adobe platforms faced with wood, packed with spectators, a noisy heated gesticulating crowd, more that of a Bourse than a racing track, very concentrated and fetid. The patrón, going by what he knew of the "stable", so to speak, and that preliminary peck, betted his hundred or two hundred soles—in one main he bet five hundred soles, what a man might earn in the highlands of Peru as a labourer after a hundred days work—and his cronies betted on a slightly lesser scale. Though the thick passage of notes, such a rare sight on the poverty-stricken puna, heightened the emotion of the occasion.

Meanwhile the spurs were being fitted. It was as leisurely as the prologue to an Arab song, interrupted by greetings, talk, the owners with the help of beeswax and thread placing the spurs in regulation position. They were workers in a clinic, surgeons' assistants, getting the right knives ready. The pointed weapons were like scimitars. They were setting the birds up as butchers, mad butchers out to carve each other. And at last it was done, this preliminary part, and an owner was walking his bird about as if to exercise him in the garden, but securely held at the end of a cord. He knelt down to him, smoothed his back. There, there, little bird, take it calmly.

The other cock was ready, the judges satisfied. Off came leather covers from the spurs, and the cord from the garden-sauntering bird. All humans out of the ring.

Pause. The birds seemed disinterested. About eight feet off, positioned sideways, pecking each at his immediate bit of earth. Sudden cockcrow, startling enough, and surge of interest among spectators. But did these birds know of each other, they were so studiously pecking at the ground, perhaps edging fractionally nearer, nearer, then scratching like bulls about to charge, then—

up they had gone, crests aloft, eagles ablaze with a first second's valour. Massacre of feathers followed. Down, and up again, exhorted by their backers, who screamed if there was any scurrying away. The patrón roared like a bull in his eagerness. Everyone, loosely speaking, was in the ring, appraising each thrust and beady peck, urging their choice to savage the throat, to gouge deeper into some wound, to disregard the bleeding tissue that had once been its own eye. Once more into the air, but a hopeless last gesture: the loser flopped, cowered, flat.

He was not even now always dead. And once or twice, for an acme of excitement, a board was dropped at this point between the birds, held almost beak to beak, then removed for a final frenzy of slaughter. That usually did the trick.

It was over. The whole afternoon was over, and it was possible to walk about again, just to look at things that were not bleeding. For days after, especially while eating, I had this impression of savaged eyes.

The patrón and company, several thousand soles richer, exuded good fellowship after the spectacle. They complained of enormous appetites, and thirst, thirst for an evening of chicha. As it was partly to entertain me, and was the occasion of handing me one or two gifts to bear securely to the Señora, and there was also, very nice of them, a present for myself, I couldn't conceivably have not gone along. It was simpler just to get as drunk as possible, and spend Monday sleeping it off. It was obviously part of the price one paid consorting with these Andean warriors.

At moments, though, I must admit I felt the price was climbing a bit too high. I felt a reaction against the family as a whole, and my journeying trailed by its apron strings. Perhaps in Cuzco I could just be a tourist.

7

CUZCO

Cuzco certainly comes at the tourist. I can't imagine anyone escaping, passing through as though it were just another town. The weather of course at this season was assisting, black clouds banked above mountains, thunder and torrential light-quelling rain, as though the chariots of the dark gods were passing; but as the clouds lifted, and the sun came through, the massive brooding nature of the place, the sheer weight of forbidding memories embodied in cyclopean walls, as if as well as the Incas and the conquistadors, the Borgias and the Tzars and more latterly the Gestapo had worked out their passions here, cut off all other impressions. And not only in the walls, though those vast grey blocks, that exquisitely shaped dungeon material both saddened and filled one with foreboding as if they controlled the town's possibilities: not only in these, but in adjacent squares, seedy and languishing with perhaps a church and a besotted beggar staring at each other, there were insistent echoes from a doleful past. Ancient Mariners in every wisp of a breeze. Not a sound say for a space of minutes, after a car had snorted through, for the passage of the barefoot peasantry was ghostlike: then suddenly the nearby tolling of a bell—though from which century was the bell tolling? The churches were resplendent within, the best rooms of this urban mausoleum, with a taste as one might have expected for agony, for carvings that writhed with spiritual torment in their dark niches, or in glass and gilt as if in an ecclesiastical Tussauds; then you came out to the streets again, turned up an Incaic passage with its grim mosaic of stone rising

as a platform now for a palace or a convent or some latter-day
conversion. Who walked those walls? Lady Macbeth?

It was like being in the final walking place of all dark spirits.

All the same I found a hotel with room and bath, and a good
table: slept well, found congenial companions. These were Latin
Americans other than Peruvians, though a few Limeñans who
could resist paying the higher price at the Tourist Hotel had
quietly found their way here. It was new, comfortable, rather like
a club, and I first fell in with an Argentine couple who spoke
over-perfect English. It became unnecessary to use Spanish, a
welcome change for I suddenly realised how circumscribed my
speech had become; and the release of ideas in my own language
convinced them, I suppose, that I was just the companion to
alleviate their own slight boredom. For they were bored with
travelling, rather bored with each other: they had not realised
before setting out how wrapt up each of them was in the routine
life of Buenos Aires. Without their habits they were a bit on
edge.

As against Limeñans they were less mannered, less subtle,
less volatile; they were highly educated, quietly polite, and they
liked to sit and talk by the hour about the wonderful city they
came from. We wandered up to the Plaza de Armas, the main, the
drilling square of Cuzco, with the Cathedral and other churches
round it, and we did these and then adjourned for a coffee and a
civilised chat. That was the way in Buenos Aires: never to go
too long without a coffee. Oh yes, they had absorbed the churches,
noted the dark tormented interiors and the quality of the picture
framing, had listened with stoical composure to a guide's recital
of the story to be gleaned from the paintings of the Loyola
family—better described, as they had known, in books: but
then, let's see, in B.A. at this hour what would they have been
doing? Would he have rung her yet from the office, joined her
at the club to discuss the scandal that had broken the night before?
Just which scandal would it have been?

This was vital; they had to debate it.

We stood again in that same Plaza, the centre, the navel of the

Inca empire, with the four highways streaming out of it—north-west to the Apurimac Bridge, Ayacucho, Huancayo, and up the cordillera to Quito; south-east through Puno to Chile; then laterally, to the coast, and to the jungle; and we re-created, before the rain burst down on us, some rough picture of barbaric splendour—of the Lord Inca with priests and captains, noble hostages and men of enterprise from all the conquered tribes of the realm (as if, say, in a scene from Aida), in full durbar to receive homage. In marched the regular legions and the conscripts, the captive slaves by the score to impress (and to pad the ceremony, as today with tanks and missile carriers), and captured artisans to be added to the gold and silver working quarter, and loot bearers, and drovers and flocks, and trumpeters and drummers, and representative chieftains from every province that worshipped the Sun, and, essential component, the temple virgins: and then next day from dawn onwards in this same square the Lord Inca officiated in the ritual of worship, bade the Sun drink and kindled the fire, and suitably finished with a golden banquet at which great goblets of chicha were consumed. In the background some score of miscreants were being strangled or thrown to wild animals.

Such was our picture, very skimpy alas beside the one ancient chroniclers portray, but my companions had soon had enough of history and were uneasy if one grew imaginative, and in any case the rain caught us, drilling down and sluicing off the eaves, and we ran straightway back to the hotel and after lunch found a fourth for bridge. This was perfectly Porteño, as those from Buenos Aires say of themselves.

Next day we continued by car, to Sacsahuaman. First a watery trip up the hill behind the town, the road at one point becoming a river and we a very agitated launch; but we bumped through, and the sky cleared, and we came to the great Inca fortress. This, on the last gentle slope of a hilltop, consisted of three jagged terraces to a total height of sixty feet, the first wall being nearly thirty feet high and over a thousand feet long, and containing, in the perfect jigsaw of pieces, one piece of over twenty tons that

measured thirty-eight feet long by eighteen high by six thick.
What a boulder! What a jigsaw! For monolith matched monolith,
fitting without mortar snugly, and sometimes to form the entire
front of a salient. It was said to have taken seventy years and
relays of tens of thousands of workmen—to hammer with stone,
for they had no iron, to roll these monoliths for miles from the
quarries, to measure and dress and lug them into place with the
help of earth mounds: but for what? Thought of as a fortress, it
seemed excessive, like building a battleship to defend a canal.
The area of course was thick with forts, alternating with priestly
hide-outs; the Incas like all overweening imperialists had an
embattled mentality. But why just here, to deter whom? Perhaps,
again as with totalitarians, they needed to feel that everyone was
occupied, that vast structures were going up. Perhaps it had
just been feeling for stone: for here, against the forbidding sky, the
forbidding stone said all that could be said for its mass and shape
and colour and surface.

We returned to town, and to more bridge, a cosy corner
through the afternoon's downpour in which to recall more
civilised places, that is to say, such as Buenos Aires.

In the evening I went for a stroll alone. I had also got talking
to a young Colombian who in turn was talking to a Venezuelan
couple, but those three from the north and the Argentines,
despite all that history had given them in common, were no
better disposed to each other than they might have been to
Bulgarians, say. "Bogota! Caracas!" The names came out,
from my bridge partners, as if referring to unseemly personalities
once again in the wrong columns of the news. They were gravely
polite when meeting in the hall; but I could not have gone for a
walk with the others, in any case of a younger generation, without
bringing a chill to this first companionship. I had secretly joined
their trip for the next Sunday, but by then the Argentines would
have left.

My stroll alone was a depressing affair. It was cold and dark,
the main square running with a score of muddy streams. At the

house corners one avoided the water still lobbing out of the gutters. Enough people were moving about, uniformed school children especially, and some boys like bats were swooping round the square on racing bicycles, and buses were leaving for villages, and shops were aglitter; but then, it seemed, on every side, in the recesses of walls, in the shadow of pillars, in doorways or simply numb in the open, squatted or slumped the human rubbish, the rejects, the figures so far beyond hope they were now outside of time too. This was the local variant of Indian of the lowest social category. One didn't ask at this point, were they labourers no longer worth their hire? Were they serfs, free men, habitual drunkards? There was no such question one could usefully ask. They were completely gone, gone from us, yet still, their skull and bone structure visible beneath adhering skin, they stayed among us, perhaps essential props for the grimly enduring masonry behind them. They were like the mummies in the museum, shrunken relics of long ago.

No point in theorising as to whether they had had it better then, as entries, so to speak, in the Inca ledgers, as participants in the disciplined uplift that at best their Indian world had given them. The point was, they had nothing now.

They fitted too well this gloomy city.

This gloomy, and definitely threatening city. They were weird harbingers of horrors to come.

Next morning I caught the train, the ordinary train not the auto-coach, down the Urubamba to Machu Picchu. It was like an old horse that occasionally cantered to stop for long gasping rests. At each of these the carriage windows were thronged with women selling food. Apart from cooked dishes there were raw vegetables, fruits, cheese; and there was a passenger opposite who bought each time, a bunch of onions or a cheese or apples, filling her straw bag with gifts, for it was clear from everything about her that she was returning home after a time in Lima. She had the metropolitan air, and station by station she was easing herself in to being a country girl again. But only for a week—

when at last I asked her; she couldn't live anywhere now but Lima.

Next to her on the narrow wood seat was a pert little chola with immense eyes, a round ball of a body in a long blue skirt with lurid petticoats, an apron, and a tall white straw hat; and opposite, her husband in overalls and shirt. They were preoccupied with the Lima girl, a very recent transformation, so that conceivably a year before she had just been a chola too: they were analysing her point by point to see wherein the difference lay. Clothes, obviously, a wider vocabulary, a brisker air already softening, reservations about country trains: and yet there was something else they couldn't place, some indefinable creole accretion that drew them to her. After my démarche they began to question her, weighted questions with silences between. When strawberries appeared the chola bought some, tossed them in her apron to pick out the best, and offered these to the picture-book girl. As their fingers met there was another difference: the perfect manicure of the coast, and the field-grubbing nails of the sierra. Poor chola, she blushed as she saw it. From that point, I bet she was converted.

Leaving the broad Anta basin, with maize and fat pigs and cattle, and horsemen casually slumped in the saddle swinging a length of rope at their herds, we plunged towards the Urubamba canyon. The first gorge closed about us, interlacing us with a chocolate torrent, grey-green boulders stacked above; our old engine enjoyed this, whistling and braking like a great express; two aged Indians crossing by a plank that ran from either bank to a rock midstream hustled back in alarm; we hurtled through. The valley of Urubamba, at its tip by Ollantaytambo, appeared: maize again, and barley, manioc, fruits and, as its name in Quechua betrays, a bad reputation for grubs. There was a profusion of flowers in the village gardens, roses and orchids, fuchsia, broom; and fields cut by willows and poplar, and behind, high above the cliffs, the cloud-dancing snow-capped peaks. We had a ten minute hissing stop, the engine imperiously impatient; then on we plunged into the canyon, sweeping almost waltzing round the bends as the sky disappeared upwards. Machu Picchu station. Tropical here, with a humid lushness; the canyon beyond was the mouth of the jungle. But now having dropped from eleven thousand feet to six thousand six hundred feet, it was necessary to ascend the cliff, by hotel bus up a zigzag track that only a producer of murder films could be happy to have hit upon, to regain a vantage of six hundred feet. This brought one to a saddle between two peaks, with the gorge coiling in a hairpin beneath, the precarious mountain-viewing platform that had been the Incas' last hide-out.

There was a good hotel. No need to rush. In fact, if one could put all the ballyhoo behind one, the tourist need to go gaga with superlatives (as the visitors' book recorded: "Greatest emotion of my life!" "Among the clouds I saw His face. Oh Holy, Holy!" "Incomparable! Gorgeous!"), it was like all slightly dizzying views with constant play of peak and cloud very stimulating to some sense within. It was nature being more rhetorical than usual, comforting for high-pitched humans (or, equally, leading them into delusions: which might have helped the Incas to fall for it), and in addition now there were these ruins, set among the near-vertical terraces that the Indians had so perfectly developed, a miniature imperial garrison town with examples of each sector in good preservation. For the archeologist, a field day; for the tourist, a double six.

Wandering round, once again it was the stonework that riveted attention. Circling walls, monolithic windows, tomblike niches, runs of steps. The gaunt grey look of the stone, its undomesticated feel to the hand: so that as the mists enveloped it, leaving below a chasm of scenery as in a Chinese painting, one wondered when they cleared if it would still be present. So hard, and yet so utterly remote, in this most isolated of settings.

At the hotel I met an English family, temporary residents of Lima. The coastal desert had been getting too much for them, their weekend memories were full of sand for they always liked to get out of the city for a romp along the Pacific beaches; so they had decided on a mountain jaunt instead. Oh, what a mistake!

They had been here three days. They had always been told they must see Machu Picchu, but their digestion was spoilt and they couldn't sleep and usually it was clammy, and it reminded them of the ghost scenes in Hamlet. The "only" hotel in Cuzco was full. The area was terribly undeveloped. The poverty was appalling. Thank God next summer they were due back in England.

At the next table a Peruvian gentleman, a professor from San Marcos University, in quite the most dotty phrases imaginable, was extolling the sacredness of the site.

One last entry from the visitors' book: "A real crazy place, man!"

Back in Cuzco, by next morning's train, I checked that the Argentines had left and went for an afternoon stroll with the Colombian. But companionship did not soften the scene. It was a drier day, and busy later on account of the big Saturday market, and so there were crowds of cholos everywhere, thriving and ruddy-faced with chicha, music—huaynos, calypsoes, tangos—lilting the afternoon along: but . . . and one apologises for always spoiling the jollity of the occasion like this . . . but the same discreditable figures, the ghastly spectres, lurked in the shadows, pitted the corners as with disease or lay slumped on the pavement edge; and others who had not so totally collapsed, who perhaps had only just come from some village, some estate or high valley community where their families were sliding into starvation, stared with that soft fathomless stare that dying animals adopt; and others, with a spark of protest left, trundled discordantly into the crowd. There was a pressure of slow seething anger both among the crowds and in silent corners. Cuzco was a darkly brooding place.

And then there were the porters, more numerous here than they had been in Ayacucho. A shopkeeper required porterage; he signalled a man recognisable by the loop of rope about his neck, exactly as with those burghers of Calais, that same condemned shaven look; the man approached, trotted up like a dog, knelt on the pavement and received the load, some overshadowing bale or

box that the rope was now used to secure, was steadied to his
feet and sped on his way. All across town they came shuffling
through, on trajectories the rest of us stepped aside from for fear
these moving towers might fall. They looked saddest, however,
while waiting to be summoned. They accepted indignity, as with
ricksha boys or culprits left in the village stocks.

Next morning, Sunday, we drove to Pisac. It was obviously
something of a tourist stunt, but it made an outing and got us
away from a politician, a henchman of Odria, who was to appear
before the people of Cuzco. The police car had been circulating
like a March hare, and armed pickets had appeared at crucial
points; and in particular this disgusted the Venezuelans, who were
highly political and who for that same reason had been critical
of the Argentines.

As the gentleman said, "It was not just Perón, but the Conservative climate that made Perón possible, with recourse, rather
than let the Radicals in, to military adventurers. It was the same
in Venezuela: Accion Democratica, from 1945 to 1948, built up
the Trade Unions, the Press, education, social security—the usual
evolutionary democratic process. So we got Jimenez. For ten
years! We got Estrada and the Guasina concentration camp.
Torture and corruption and national bombast. The same, I
believe, Señor, in Colombia . . . ?"

The Colombian assented. "Though I was about to say that the
process in Argentina and in your country, Señores, was not,
not . . ."

"Of course. Differences. But underlying—"

"Yes. And even more pronounced with us. It was precisely the
reluctance of the Conservatives, 'les pájares', as we say, to cede
power to the Liberals, 'les chusmeros', that brought in Pinilla in
1953. We endured four years of him and of that. Though the
strife continues. Thousands each year are killed in every province.
Conservatives do not easily give up!"

He had a beautiful smile and he bestowed this on the lady, who
managed, without saying a word at this point, to seem to be

leading the conversation. All these Latin Americans were relaxed, adroit, skipping ahead of themselves.

"And of course Peru! Peru . . . !" The Venezuelan raised his hand in despair. Peru, in a fairly sick continent, was quite the sickest number for him. "This man Odria! The Peronistas helped him. To foment disorder, the Communists also. As with Jimenez, as with Batista—none of us have so greatly diverged. Our sad self-lacerating continent!"

He continued: "This Odria ruled from 1948 to 1956—only two years less than Jimenez, so perhaps these changes are a matter of fashion!—and, principally, he outlawed APRA. You will recall, Señor, that for four years Haya de la Torre took refuge in your Embassy. He outlawed APRA which I think is the equivalent of our Accion Democratica."

"Well . . ." My voice.

"He outlawed APRA. Like all generals, he favoured building schemes. Grandiose schemes. Foreign investment. Like Jimenez, he did not himself grow poorer." The Venezuelan paused, purring over this, licking his chops at the wickedness of it. "So he had to go; and he will not come back: whatever the generals in Washington say. Those Jimenez-Batista-Trujillo-loving generals. Our continent is getting wiser."

"So who do you say will govern Peru?" My voice again, arching round from the front offside position. The Colombian was next to me, the Venezuelans at the back next to the Cuzqueñan guide. After Pisac we were continuing to Ollantaytambo to look at the Inca fort there, making a day of it. They were leaving on the morrow.

"After the next elections? If the army doesn't jump in before-hand?" The Venezuelan pondered. "It should be Haya. Just look what Betancourt is doing for us. Education and agriculture to the fore again. And these gentlemen also have learned from exile to be more-er . . . cautious; there's no harm in that. Who else, Señor Sykes? Do you suggest, the British Navy?"

"Good heavens, no."

But how they loved the little joke, how antiquated their picture of Britain.

"You see, finally, it returns to this: with all his faults it has to be Haya—or Ramiro Priale who's behind the scenes—or else the Communists sweep the board. As in all our countries, the Conservatives must choose."

His wife was shuddering at the thought of the Communists. "We had such nice friends in Havana." She lit a cigarette. Her husband did too. For a moment it looked as if we might discuss Cuba, where those Conservatives had sat the fence too long. But abruptly interest flagged, there was a pause as if to don other costumes and make-up. Then they were talking of the work of Henry Moore. They had just added to their own collection.

Monday morning, my companions gone, and the feeling that I ought to meet someone local. Tourism was wearing thin. Though I had felt excited too at their plans for flying on from Lima to Saõ Paulo, a mere seven hours to cross the continent, and from there to explore the new capital, Brasilia. And their liberal concerned approach to these countries, which ultimately they hoped would federate, seemed also to leave a window open here. Conditions in Cuzco had been seen by them, and seen as a Latin American problem; these wretches, even the Bronze Age spectres, by that much were the less alone. As the Colombian had said, these private hells were being ventilated bit by bit, and men of like mind throughout the continent were beginning to feel they had to combine to put their joint house in order.

"As a matter of fact, though it's heresy to say it, and I do not talk like this at home, the interim solution is birth control. If Castro comes up first with that one! I tell you, Señores," and he had turned to the others, "if the Church cannot argue us through it, she will have failed our continent in this century."

But the Venezuelans had declined the gambit.

On my own again I found my letters of introduction and set off to deliver them. The first took me to a patrician mansion and a bell beside a thick timber gate locked and double-bolted.

Repeated ringing brought no reply. A tailor opposite and a street lounger both encouraged me to keep on trying; so I did, and eventually footsteps sounded and a voice enquired who I was. Like Pyramus through the wall to Thisbe, except that there was no cranny, I explained; but the footsteps receded; then others came, high-heeled instead of slouching sandal, and the interrogation proceeded. At last with much grating and wheezing of metal an inch of gate was pulled back, so that I could see a courtyard and a loggia above it, and above, the steep wall rising to a roof. Cobbles, plants, and grandiloquent stone. Then the girl revealing at least one eye told me her master was not at home, took the letter and closed the gate.

Back in the Cuzco street as before.

Next I dealt with the second letter, addressed to a friend of Azuarga, who was a young poet and a middle-aged lecturer and quite an old family man—Azuarga's description. I was to look for him at the University. There, a sorry place indeed, like an impoverished Mechanic's Institute, they said I should find him at a certain high school. At the high school, on tenterhooks because army officers were examining the boys, the headmaster was assuring me in no time, felt called upon seemingly to tell me, that Cuzco was a Catholic town without a single Communist in it. Robles? Certainly. But my dear sir, please do me the ineffable honour of sitting down for a few minutes' talk. Please do me, as a visitor, as a traveller from afar, the incalculably sublime favour of seating yourself for a word or two. Robles? My dear sir, he isn't here today. Now please, most gracious, most esteemed . . .

At the Prefecture, another clue, they decided that he had gone to Lima; but they kindly gave his home address. I found him there, near the University, in a neat little dwelling on a housing estate built by General Odria, romping on the carpet with three children. Hardly bothering to read the letter—"Azuarga? Perfect. Please come in"—he added me to his afternoon, that one quickly guessed had in fact included the other duties and appointments, and could take in a dozen more, layer upon layer to be slipped away from as the next one crossed his mind. He was around thirty, slight, dynamic, a bantam figure who could control a crowd with a wiry word or the right piece of knowledge. He was high diving in among the children.

He slid round to mention of Eliot. Shaking off drops of children's play he extolled the Peruvian poet Vallejo. Could I read Greek, to help with his Cavafy? Spanish? How good really was my Spanish—not good enough, he feared, for Vallejo. As neither was his English for Dylan Thomas.

He offered me a drink. We were in comfortable chairs. Poetry dispensed with, except that casually he had signed and handed me a book of his own verse, we had moved on to travel. Russia, China . . . these were the giants of the future. He had recently been with a group to China, examining that extraordinary experiment; he had published his findings, but for a minority public. Here in Peru to speak of Marxism was to trade the public hieroglyphics. Even those who openly professed it or looked to it as their salvation were as often as not local intriguers or sections of the depressed masses blindly following a standard of revolt. Without a break-through in education . . . he shrugged . . . one needed to be very cynical.

He was smiling to himself, and so was I. At one point he had admitted he was a Communist, at the next to become a detached observer. His wife entered now, blonde, white-skinned, as febrile and adroit as he; like him she had a series of jobs, so that between them they owned the car outside, and I learned later he owned a bit of land leased to a smallholder. All these intellectuals owned land. For not to own land or have a stake in land was to belong to the very poorest category, the Indian serf on the ranch's books, the semi-slave of the jungle plantation, or the same type swelling the city barriadas. And that level was not yet articulate.

All the same, as he was shortly informing me, a good three-quarters of the usable terrain of Peru was owned by large proprietors, something less than two per cent of the people, as throughout Latin America. On the coast where statistics were better kept (he consulted a paper 2·08 per cent of the actual owners held 77·15 per cent of the cultivable land, and of these a mere seventy-nine held 50 per cent of the cultivable land, that is 356,426 hectares (a hectare being 2¾ acres) dividing to an average 7128·5 hectares each, except that a handful of proprietors held most of this; while the smallholders, 97·92 per cent, held an average 1·98 hectares each.

Up here on the sierra, my friend, it was worse, for how many thousands owned nothing at all; and despite the talk of Agrarian Reform the large estates were constantly growing. Just growing, for the sake of that satisfaction. For areas of them were never touched, stretched idle endlessly into the hills; and taxes were evaded, so the yield was nil. While the land hungry peasants starved, or migrated to the coast, or, as now, struck—

As I nodded, to show I had caught his meaning, his wife thrust in, "So you have heard, Señor? It has always happened that there have been these raids between ranches and Communists, burning barns and stealing livestock; such country warfare has never stopped. But what begins now is more significant. The peasants are forming Sindicatos; their discontent is being organised. These latest re-occupations of land are a warning to the nation."

She scuttled the children off to supper; and Robles took up the theme, shaping it differently even as he touched it to give prominence to his native Cuzco. What happened in Cuzco today, he affirmed, coloured the soul of Peru for a decade. It was the Indian not the creole city, however wealthy that other might be, or however fast it sucked in people, that was the true pulsating heart of the country.

Was he right in this? I very much wondered. But he persisted: the Indian population was again six million as in the time of the Incas (though by 1770, a rough halfway between Pizarro's landing and the present time, it had been cut, through war, slavery, disease, to seven hundred thousand); and education, etc. for the Indian would not necessarily turn out another Western man; for the Indian, if one day he ruled, might feel an absolute inward necessity to cast off all that had borne upon him—of which Lima was one symbol—since the time of the Conquistadors. The iniquities suffered, the stunning cruelty, the darkening over of all his sky: it was this that completely conditioned him still. Too early to see beyond that.

Robles added, "I am sure of this . . . the unexpected, and the strange, will happen."

"Let me tell you a story," he said some minutes later. I had given him my impressions of Cuzco and I had also shown him the newspaper cutting that had so appalled me at the first in Lima, the details of whippings on an estate near Cuzco. "Oh yes," he had replied, "we all know him. But that is not an isolated case. Conditions throughout the Valle de la Convención are sickeningly medieval. Another scandal that is cooking up, so that the police will have to do something about it, is the local slave traffic in children—minors, that is, under eighteen years delivered by the father for a hundred soles and the promise of good pay to follow, smuggled by train or bus to La Convención by the slavers, 'los enganchadores', and there forced to work, and forgotten. Forgotten, that is, unless they escape or are foolish enough to stage a revolt, or, as recently join the Movimiento Communal. This Movement, you see, is another arm of the new awakening among the Indians. It intends to appeal to the United Nations citing the abuses that you have read about. It could cite a hundred more. All Cuzqueñans can. Every man in the highlands can. These barbarities are commonplace, north or south."

"Add that," he had continued, "to the facts concerning land. How six estates in La Convención between them—take one estate alone in the Department of Puno!—own over three hundred thousand hectares. While all the Communities throughout Peru, about four thousand last pockets of freedom, cannot together total half a million hectares, of usable terrain, for the support of their three to four million Indians. From which they are still being ousted! So they strike back! They occupy land—in advance of the much talk-of Reform. Which Reform they do not believe in, be it from Haya or Belaunde, because of the debate about how to pay for it. That is the position, net, Señor."

He had gone on, fiery in his anger now—"Poor whipped dogs, were they never to turn! Were they always to work the fields till they dropped, or be pushed back to stones for soil? You can still see, today in Cuzco, Indian serfs in the households of their masters, who have walked five days from the feudal estate to fulfil their term of unpaid service in the equally feudal establishment here. Pongo, it's called. Tyrants need it. As much as anything, it's psychological. And all this creates the atmosphere of Cuzco, the tortured threatening gloom you sensed. Cuzco mirrors its countryside, it mirrors what happens behind its walls; and the rest of Peru catches reflections. Peru cannot but mirror Cuzco. In sum, a haunting blood-stained image!

Let me tell you a story . . ."

He now grew calm, speaking in a soft rapid voice, his hands giving little flips of emphasis. "In the time of the Viceroys it was even worse; I will say that, it was even worse. The people oppressed by extortions, 'los repartos', and thinned out by forced labour. So that eventually, in 1780, an Indian cacique, who had been schooled by the Jesuits and was a man of culture, and who claimed to be a descendant of the Incas, took the great name of Tupac Amaru and proclaimed revolt. Thousands flocked to him. He executed the Corregidor of Tinta, a foul oppressor, and marched on Cuzco. Unfortunately he delayed attacking; he relied first on treaty and reason. So the Spaniards gained time, began inflicting defeats, and finally captured Amaru and his family.

"Then, on Friday, 18th May 1781, in the square here, they took vengeance. Four minor captains were hung at once. The other six Indians were tied in sacks and dragged to the square centre by horses. Two of them, Amaru's uncle and a son, had their tongues cut out and were garrotted, together with another cacique, by iron screws. Next came Michaela, the wife of the Inca: for her the same treatment, but as her neck was too small she was finished off by tugs of a lasso. At last, Tupac Amaru himself. His tongue was cut, and then he was tied by lassos to four horses, that pulled in four different directions to tear him: but this also was inadequate, for he stayed in the air like a horrible stretched spider, so the judge had him beheaded. His child Fernando, of ten years, who had watched this horror and shrieked his heart out, was condemned to life imprisonment. Heads, bodies, limbs of the victims were stuck up on as many poles, to remind Cuzco of who was master, and circulated through the countryside . . . they say a great wind and storm arose. . . .

"Now I, dear Señor, when I walk in the square, can never completely dismiss that scene. Can any of us here, can Cuzco itself? There were afterwards other scenes of execution but that was the most frightful one. At the centre of the square, the very centre, the navel of the Inca world . . . do you see?

"Let's hope, let's hope . . ." He broke off swiftly as his wife re-entered to offer supper.

Ham, eggs, toast, cheese: he didn't notice what he was eating. He would be leaving soon for a conference in Chile; he had some standing as a historian. He was interested in English social welfare. He would like to see the churches in Florence. The cathedrals of France. Spain. Portugal. So little time. Well, everyone knew it.

No time, no time, so much to be accomplished.

Sometimes, even, one marked time deliberately!

And off he went again, the thought of time biting him, into the exigencies of politics. There, and he glimmered with a swift sly smile, was a sphere in which one ate one's heart out. And because that didn't suit the Latin temperament look at the follies committed! Suicides! Contortions, acrobatics—call them what you liked! A sphere in which the tortoise won.

What did he personally think of APRA? Si, Señor. Pinned to the particular he was about to slide on, then paused, as if for another set of keys, fingered them, spoke: "APRA, si." He deliberately, smiled at his wife. How to put it on this occasion? Suddenly he was off at speed again.

"For instance, Señor, there are two big parties, APRA and Accion Popular, but both set up to fight the wars, or elections, of thirty years ago. This can't last; everyone knows it; so we all now look beyond the Election. The leaders cry that they will not bargain, that alliances between them are ruled out: but this is

simply to establish for the record how many votes each gets alone
—honestly, and dishonestly, Señor—and thus to establish their
relative strengths for the real, post-Election settlement. A mar-
ginal possibility is that the economic oligarchy, disillusioned with
Beltran, will support Odria; but without the army they can't
stem the tide. And the tide is set for moderate reform.

So . . . we get either APRA or AP, one of the two big omnibus
parties. For each contains right-wing elements, not dissimilar, and
left-wing elements stretching as far left as the Communists, not
always of course self-proclaimed. How to choose? Does it matter?
The results will be running neck to neck. And, whoever wins, if
he tries to rule alone through feelings of personal exclusiveness,
will then fall prey to his own left-wing, abetted at that point by
the other party just to see what mischief can be done. Next step,
inevitably, will be the entry, through fear of radicalism, of
military pressure: either to stiffen the ruling leader into the
facsimile of dictatorship, or to throw him out and put the other
leader in, if that other one seems a more likely caudillo.

Good! All this turns on exclusiveness, on vendetta—Haya's
feelings, Belaunde's feelings.

But . . . suppose they come to an arrangement? Common sense
requires it. Both need to shed their extreme left-wing, and to
unite against the economic oligarchy. For APRA it finally rids
them of Prado, and perhaps of military distrust; for AP it gives an
opening into the APRA-controlled Sindicatos. Not a bad bargain,
no? It's obvious. It would give Peru a modern party of the middle,
and the beginnings of peaceful evolution. The dissidents of the
left could also unite . . . in fact, seeing this, they are beginning to
do so. Politics require these deaths and births. In twenty years
time, other alignments"

"That's the most cheering forecast I've heard." I was wonder-
ing where he stood in all this.

He was smiling quietly, resting his analysis, perhaps tying it up
here and there in his mind. His wife was smiling to herself too. I
had still the suspicion that they were less detached than appeared

from this sweetness of presentation, but he had clearly said all he ment to say.

Now also it was time to be moving; a glance at his watch implied other appointments. In a flash we were disentangled from the house, and from the neat little housing estate, and bowling uptown in their car. He dropped me at the door of my hotel.

"Si, Señor, it is as I have told you—if events move logically! But in Peru can that possibly happen? Is not logic here bent by destiny? Think of what I have told you of Cuzco . . . of its baneful history . . . of that sense of its waiting only the more fiendishly to strike back! You have sensed it yourself. So, you see? It's not just a poetic idea. Adios, Señor!"

But I saw him again. Always speeding round town in his car. He waved, dashed on; sometimes stopped for a word. These were encounters for odd moments in the car, quite the strangest I have ever had, but which seemed to go with his temperament. The talk took up where he had dropped it before, a continuum re-established by some flick of a switch. "As I say, this development comes too late! Too late, past its moment in time. Peru no longer can wait for evolution. The starving peasant is pressed, Señor . . ."

". . . I think you wish me to speak optimistically? Rationally? Like some good bourgeois who sleeps with his conscience." He smiled. I obviously was his bourgeois. "But all that is out of key in Peru, except for political pamphleteering. It is a hell, an inferno, on the edge of which we sit so lightly talking. There is hardly anything of anything, food, shelter, education, that you take for granted. Consult the statistics compiled by the international bureaux. Please . . ."

". . . So what will happen at the first improvement? When more daylight floods in to the peasant? Will he use it for sweet reasonableness? No. No, Señor. He will use it better to take aim by, to string the bourgeois up by. And to string up any onlooker too. For it is only through blood, through thick blood, that Peru can obey its destiny and at last, as a nation, not a feudal preserve, discover its own mode of advance. And only the party that gives rein to this . . . has any relevance today, Señor."

"You mean the Communists?"

He shrugged. "Naturally. Though the first stage might be . . . Odria."

The last time I saw him he seemed to have regretted proceeding so logically to this conclusion. "You understand, I speak as a poet. Blood is a word we like to use. Logic is something we play about with. But you are right, Señor, to reprove me with this: there is no future along such a path. Common sense must win. Even now at this minute I am on my way to an APRA meeting . . . or, let me see, is it an AP meeting?" He grinned slyly. "I have my work to do. Adios, very good Señor!"

He disappeared, attuned to destiny.

Complementary to this was my other encounter. Back at the hotel a note awaited me that in its flourish and courtesy belied the reception at the bolted gate. Could I be there at four next day? Stirred by Robles to a sense of drama about to explode from these brooding uplands I was keen to see how the other side viewed it, to take a peep within the battlements; and the thin florid writing suggested a querulous entertaining old gentleman; and then he was Paula's uncle, by her first marriage (she included him as an uncle), and it was three weeks since I had seen her in Lima and it would be pleasant to feel in contact again, to be in a house where she had often visited. In fact if his note had not been waiting I should have taken the next plane to Lima. I missed the creole city, my temporary home.

The gate stood open. The overslanting eaves threw shadows across the walled approach, but the gate itself had been thrown back as if for a troop of horse to enter. There was a first small door, a porter's room, where an individual stood watching, but no sooner had he moved towards me than as if by some countermanding signal a woman, of higher standing in the household, in European dress and cardigan and short white socks and shoes, appeared at the far side of the courtyard, checked and motioned me towards the stairway. I mounted, taking in the solidity of this well holed with surrounding doorways from which if need be retainers could spring and decimate attacking forces, while above the loggia's slender colonnade came more peacefully into view; and there at the top another individual quizzed me only to be brushed aside, and his master, the laird himself stood welcoming —a horny gaze, a dry handclasp.

He motioned me ahead. It was becoming more domestic. Below, the pit was softened from here by the feathery tops of giant grasses and a bushy kind of climbing plant against the white-washed stone; above, on the roof, birds had paused; while here in the gallery there was a Tyrolean charm of balustrade and potted geraniums and ornately carved doors and ceiling. There were one or two chairs, a carved settee, and some spongy-looking ottomans: perhaps harking back to official occasions in family or local history or to an era of overflowing entertainment; and in recesses of the walls there was floral tiling and, in one or two, gilt-framed mirrors, fronted by potted cacti and ferns, as if generations of housekeepers had each unthinkingly dumped one there.

We entered a room; this was really magnificent. Ducal in proportions, long and high, dark from the amount of cedar in chairs, console tables, screens, cabinets, and from the arabesque of the window grilles, yet light from the white-papered walls and from the ceiling divided into a checkerboard of coats of arms and golden squares, and from the sun filtering gauzily in. There was colour in the cushions, of tapestry design, or they could have been made from old ponchos, a light brown colour in the alpaca carpets, and a golden glow from a Cuzqueñan saint framed and hanging in one corner. But all these were only first points of reference, for the room was a veritable museum.

My host the laird, still guarded in expression, and moving cautiously among his possessions, a little as if to apologise to them for introducing an unknown presence, motioned me to the only comfortable chair. He had a medium fairly thickset figure, with a slight stoop that pulled up his jacket, part of the shooting tweeds he was wearing; he had elegant expressive fingers, and a thin high reticent voice, and after the usual formalities that almost exhausted all there was to say, so bland was his acceptance of my being in Peru, of my knowing Paula, of my being in his house, he muttered some excuse and disappeared through an end door into a further room.

Don Jaime gone, I surveyed the domain. One would have had to have been an auctioneer's apprentice to have noted it all down at a glance; there was the casual residue of centuries. I remarked first some ivory pieces, of Virgin and Child, and the Holy Family, certainly of Chinese manufacture, a reminder of where else the Spaniards had wandered; and getting up to look at these I stopped at a table that was a small showcase, filled with decorated silver spoons whose handles were long shawl pins, with bronze nails and knives, and a group of figurines, silver alpacas and copper llamas and a human figure, all so finely done with a quirky sort of humour to them, that I guessed these were authentic Inca; and then against the wall was an Inca aryballus, a three-foot waterjar to be roped to some poor carrier's back; and I had just got to this, and at the same time, so much was there to absorb at once, to a shelf of fine colonial plate—or rather, wasn't it all pre-Conquest, Tiahuanaco with those puma eyes?— when the laird reappeared and took the show over.

The fact that I was sniffing seemed to please him; if I was interested, so, tentatively, was he. He indicated other feline motifs, on a single-spout Cupisnique jar, on a fragment of a Pucara pitcher, as decoration to an Inca bowl. But generally the Incas, in this lovely red ware, had preferred geometric decoration, diamonds and triangles, small squares, frets and steps, everything precise, painted in clear black and white, and red. They had never suppressed story-telling, however, or reminders of the natural world, as witness their distinctive chicha beakers, of wood, kero, a small collection of which he would happily show me in the adjoining room.

On then, in his wake, more jaunty now as he was able to share his habitual promenade from one rare piece to another; and it was almost with enthusiasm, or was it with a perfectly controlled pride, that he indicated, on the row of keros, the variation in story incident—look there, warriors with bow and arrow, there an aryballus carrier, there an Inca in his palanquin, there birds and bees, and llamas of course: decoration such as earlier cultures had already perfected on cloths and pots. Though that was not to belittle the Incas. It was a pity they had not been handled more tactfully. Soldiers, alas; the passions of conquest. Though not only soldiers had come from Spain: there had been fine priests, urists, scholars. Despite the Inquisition there had been local culture. No policy of mass extermination—he challenged me, suavely, the Anglo-Saxon, the contrasting picture of Red Skin hunts flashing momentarily across our minds (except of course that there had been William Penn): but he changed it as quickly, hand on my arm, not allowing me to utter a word, into a continuing invitation to see yet more of his fine collection. Which would take us into yet another room.

The one we were in was a small study, brought lock, stock, and barrel one would have said from Spain, the room of an early scholar-romancer, geographer-astronomer, man of affairs, who conceivably had invested in Pizarro's expeditions, followed here and left this room to his descendants. He of the twirling moustaches in the portrait hung above the faded globe. The rest was leather, bound volumes, swords, and the overflow of works of art. The present Don Jaime Horcaz y Areval might have been the one to introduce those. They were obviously his passion.

The room we entered was softer, dressed in velvet and vicuña and brocade; there were pieces of Meissen, and Sèvres plate; water-colours, oil daubs; and crystal chandeliers to make the evenings sparkle. It was a room for feminine entertainment, but quietened, hushed as for a siesta, and indeed this had been his wife's drawing room, Doña Teresa, some years dead. He matter-of-factly made reference to her, his eyes skirting the portraits on the wall; but standing in the dainty glassed-in balcony, the mirador, that overlooked a side street, something stirred him and he returned to the room. He took up position before a cabinet. Sir, it was this he had wished to show me. His voice had an even blander edge to it.

He paused; then with fine fingers he took from the cabinet, as if selecting pearls from a tray, three little figures in polychrome wood, the Three Kings of the Nativity, their robes tooled and painted with the most delicate exactness, their faces expressing wonder and piety, and he revolved them slowly for each point to be noted. To them he added a Santa Rosa of Lima, a tiny figure of a nun with Baby Jesus in her arms, her expression rapt, her robe full of roses—the figure that Macú had told me, over tea, enthusing on the place of the Divine in our lives, meant more to her than mother and father. Last, from another compartment he withdrew a box, a doll's theatre that for all its darker colourings and tiny inset mirrors and decoration of vines and angels, at once recalled Don Joaquin's work, the mestizo sculptor I had met in Ayacucho. Opened up, there was a tiny stage, but none of the drama of "Las Pasiones"; only Mary and the sleeping Jesus, every detail beautifully wrought, she passing the time making lace, a cat and pigeons at her feet.

Don Jaime listened when I mentioned Ayacucho; he knew of the school, but then he waved it aside; it lacked, sir, the fineness of theme, the ethereality (I should explain, we had been speaking entirely in English), the distance, if he could phrase it like that, of these eighteenth century Quito figures. Quito, I must appreciate, had been the Sienna of the New World. An ancestor of his had been an Abbot there, as another had been its provincial governor. Links along the highlands had been strong: as indeed, already in Inca times; for Quito had been their second capital. No such fine pieces as these had been produced this far to the south. Though one could, yes one could trace a line, at least in details of decoration, from the earliest pre-Conquest ceramics and weaving through mestizo wood and stone carving to some of the popular trifles of today. One could; but one didn't need to do so. With these pieces, this authentic past, in one's hand.

In such mood, then, serene, beatific, the mood of connoisseurs that is almost mystical, of scholars who for a moment own the world like a book open before them, the laird led back to the first room where afternoon tea had been brought on a tray. At first it seemed unworthy to eat: surely there was more in that vein to be said, uncloyed by salmon sandwiches or toast? It seemed not. His temper was changing. Sugar had been omitted from the tray. He snapped as a servant answered his call. He didn't ring for the servant, he called out, and a faithful Indian padded in; an Indian, for the occasion, dressed in shoes and white shirt and black trousers and white cotton gloves.

Don Jaime's ageing polished face, freckled and frowning, was less serene. Had he had enough abruptly of my presence, or enough of these rooms he had to live in, or of the disconnection between past and present that cropped up to spoil his pleasures? He fidgeted, controlled it, frowned. I tried Paula as a possible soother. Ah, Paula. He had been meaning to tell me: he expected her any day. She liked the house, sat everywhere painting, then went out to the hacienda. There was a room there full of her work. He hoped I would be staying long enough to meet her: could I, perhaps, come to lunch on Friday? There was good trout at this time of year. Ah, yes . . . his thin high voice trailed off; a dry glimmer of a smile replaced it. Each age had its standards. His remained in the past.

I presumed he was still referring to art.

He was restless again, an increasing tremor at the edge of his bland composure. He was not himself taking any tea. I was remembering with surprise, after the studious half-hour, that he also was a haciendado, the owner of an immense hacienda and I couldn't say how many humble souls (Paula, my informant, had been offhand, but "essential for your researches", she had put it); and now suddenly I saw a chance to view another stretch of the front line, perhaps, with trouble brewing, the nearest yet to the naked heart of the battle; but as quickly I was ashamed, for after all I was his guest, and, devoted to collecting and aesthetic studies, he might be the mildest most compliant of landlords. One wondered, though, looking closely at the laird.

My thoughts rushed away: Paula coming! As restless now as he, I stood up to go.

But I had to wait a minute longer. The servitor had entered, there were shadows in the loggia, four hunched-together Indian shadows. It was something urgent. The laird shot out. He received them, listened for a second or so, enough for his face to darken over, then waved them aside to await his pleasure; though not before each had kissed his hand, an observance he plainly didn't notice. He didn't too well seem to notice them. Humble voices. Shadows. He returned to the style and the interest of this room, controlled himself perfectly and showed me out. Down the great stairway to the baronial gate. Adieu, sir, then, till Friday.

So that meant I must fill in three days. For the first time since I had entered Peru, seven weeks previously, the pressure of encounters and learning went slack. I wrote up my notes, read Cieza de León, and spent some hours each day in the retreat where Father D. was schooling catequistas. Not because of that activity, but because with the increasing burden of misery and incipient violence this land shifted on to one, that even as a traveller one could not shrug off, I felt badly the need of some hours of retreat, so as not altogether to forfeit charity, nor to lose sight of the universal involvement in cancerous situations like this. Most of us, when not taking practical measures, benefit from some such mditation.

So three days passed, that became four, as a note from Don Jaime postponed the lunch, and I began from another side to get agitated over the question, was Paula in Cuzco? I can hardly set down all my conjectures. I was perhaps more excited over her arrival than conventionally it was decent to be. My daily route went close to their mansion; it was hardly by chance she should choose to come now. I could sense something of her speculative nature.

Saturday midday, but as yet not a word. I hurried once more to the sombre gates, and was astonished to find them shut, bolted. But this was an error, quickly righted; though with a side stage fury echoing up to the master that appeared in turn to render him purple. In a minute it became embarrassingly exaggerated. He snapped away from our first few words, returned to the gallery, glowered at his henchmen, who were still softly expostulating senior to junior in the background. "Go!" They went.

But as soon as I had come to terms with the fact that Paula was not here in Cuzco, had early that morning wired an excuse, I began, paying more attention to him, to see that Don Jaime's anger had little to do with my reception. It simmered up from a deeper source. He manifestly didn't wish to discuss it, yet could not forbear from throwing out phrases, that bit by bit, perhaps through feeling for form, drove him to be more explicit.

"It is simply because of the Election," he fretted; "more Communist manoeuvres!" . . . "I do not see how a gentleman like Prado can countenance elections at this moment" . . . "Into the hands of agitators when all we require is stable rule" . . . "What is to be gained by changing teams . . . ?"

His voice went higher. He waved me to a chair. After each phrase he calmed, controlled himself, then out came more exasperation. He tried stroking a Tiahuanaco bowl. He moved disconsolately about.

He sat down. "Sir I imagine you think you are visiting a peaceful country. That this ancient land is without trouble. No, sir. I regret to say. For instance, bordering my hacienda this week, some-er people, that as it happens for years have bothered me— oh, to sell land to them, or to let them pilfer my cattle as they choose—were suddenly found armed to the teeth. A community of so-called peaceful Indians! We got warning. The Guardia Civil was sent by truck early the other morning. They unearthed a cache of arms and ammunition; and it seemed that these-er people had been receiving lessons as guerrilla fighters. You can imagine my discomposure. I sometimes stay for a week out there. Each year I speak personally to my labourers. But now—one has only to think of Bolivia! And I do not refer to the siege of La Paz, that monstrous affair, in 1781; but to recently, 1952, a revolution brought on by elections! As I say, this is the work of

agitators, assisted by democratic folly. I am convinced, sir, that it
will end badly."

As if ashamed to be admitting this, flawing the surface of
hospitality, he pressed a large whisky and soda on me, and
swallowed a double one himself. He had already been drinking
and he was not quite cutting the detached figure of the other day.
It was not through lack of courage, he had the blood of generals,
but through dismay and fury, largely helpless fury, fury at having
to watch and wait while the order of things was upset from below.
Thanks to a pack of fools in Lima. The unearthing of arms had
brought it home to him. Investigations, he assured me, were proceeding, but there seemed to be nothing he personally could do.
Except (he didn't say this) relate it to a stranger, cushioning it in
inoffensive terms. While in truth. . . .

Moreover—and this he said—none of this activity was natural
to the Indian. He prided himself he knew them well. They had
been worked upon, fooled . . . though, how now could one
ever again trust them? This too put him out of humour.

"Sir," he had again replenished our whiskies, "those who know
could tell you that the Indian from time immemorial has been
prey to fear. He is pursued by spirits and by hot forces that come
like a wind from the glacial peaks. Against them there is not too
much he can do, except, what we have taught him, to trust in
God. The Cross has become his great protection. Still, he remains
an insecure creature, walking a hostile path through life. It is
this rather than Inca overlord or Spanish conqueror or our present society that has oppressed him. I mark my words. It is not
often said. I am, perhaps . . . unfashionable in saying it."

He smiled to himself, whimsically, the absurdity of fashion
entering into such discussion. But patiently, an old man who
knew, he would continue.

"You see, sir, the Indian distrusts the universe; he is not even
too sure of his neighbour. Outside of his family he is always on
guard. I grant, there are protective alliances, of compadres, and
in the varayoq—that is, the indigenous system of officials; but his
chief characteristic is that he fears . . . so fears to offend or to

arouse trouble. If he does, in a quarrel or a rage against fortune, as soon as he is calmer he becomes frightened. Fear, fright, they call it susto: that is the terrible ruler of these people. To the extent that they would rather crouch down and be humble, and in fights feel safer when losing.

So you see, sir—they turned to chiefs or patróns. It is fundamental. We are a form of insurance. And in respect to their precarious economy we also offered material security—that is, free pasture, a strip each of land, free firewood, grain for chicha, fiesta gifts, and some slight wages of food and coca for the half week they work for us. I know, we take their labour; but this they give gladly, for apart from rewards they are being protected. That underlies other rights and obligations. That is the basis of a stable system. And also, being human yet not of their world, we are a safer target for their bursts of anger! Oh, I understand those people, I think. But the agitators don't! In a way it is the Indian, in all this subversion, who has fooled the Communist!"

He broke off, humoured by this thought, that gave a more satisfying depth to the problem. The surface of politics could be better discussed, leaving his understanding unsullied. And yet, and yet . . .

Don Jaime pondered. He was calmer now, composed again; there was nothing like philosophising to calm one. Yet a steelier glint was appearing in his eye. Those neighbouring Indians, perhaps some of his own, had been conspiring against him, the laird. The score was not yet even; they must be taught a lesson. Then, everything could be as before.

I surmise this from the talk that followed, the immediate talk over lunch. He was from moment to moment moving forward within himself to an acceptable solution; although, right through, he never ceased to give the hurt exasperated looks of a man properly engaged in connoisseurship, in elegant moments in library and salon, suddenly forced to consider his estates. It was as if the stock exchange had failed him. His whole life had been based on trust, and bang, someone had acted out of character. Perfidious

Indians! No, just a few of them. It was those few he must get his hands on.

The meal itself returned us largely to suave appreciation. Fresh turtle soup, trout, turkey; his very problems gave us appetite: and full bellies and the wine made simpler what he should do in the days ahead. Really, wouldn't it be best to forget it, to turn once more to some fragments of pottery that he believed, when pieced, would be a revelation? Keen, he enlarged upon the subject; then brought to the table an Inca "paccha", or ceremonial drinking vessel, that was one of the gems of his collection.

No good. In a pause, a minute later, he was remarking that trouble had also broken out on the ranches of the Cerro de Pasco Corporation, and on a neighbouring hacienda that he knew, to the north of Huancayo, the previous Sunday. Trouble all along the highlands! And the serious thing was it was barely a month since the last raids had been beaten back there.

"Oh yes," I began, "I heard about them."

But he raised his head. It was his train of thought. It was his anxiety, after all. For it was reading about the other disturbance, almost simultaneous with his own near shave, that had caused him so furiously to think about them, to ponder the possible scale of subversion, and to decide that punishment was called for. Yes, punishment. By the Government, of course. Though now, as he thought about it again . . .

"You see, sir, since 1957 the Community of Yanahuanca has been going to law to test its claim to parts of this hacienda I'm mentioning. Of course, the claim was not valid. Uchumarca has belonged to these people I know for at least the last hundred years. So what does the Community decide on next? To invade! War. Can we allow that?"

The laird had a very thin moustache. He gave it as best he could a twirl.

"If I was the proprietor of Uchumarca, or of Pacoyán of the American company, I think, at this point, I should teach them a lesson. A sharp once-and-for-all lesson! Ancient justice was always swift. If they invade, so should I; and strip and burn in the same fashion. Deaths would result, but our floods cause thousands, Carnival alone claims a score of victims. Death is not in this calculation. Forgive me, sir. I distress you. But I see, I am beginning to see that the solution is punishment. Stiff punishment. Though the long-term solution, as the Communities crumble, is the reciprocal contract of landlord and labourer. As I was explaining to you before."

As earlier, exposition eased his mind, and we took our coffee in a gentler mood. Some decision had framed itself for him, some instructions that with a straightened out conscience he could telephone through to his steward. But then, as so often happens when we have prepared ourselves to give a signal, the signal came to him. The phone rang. The police had a message. They had been obstructed in their duties while searching his estate. Arms had been fired at them. There was considerable disorder.

On the Community lands? he pleaded. No? No, they meant on his own hacienda? Yes, he would come there at once, personally.

In clipped removed tones he told me. He was aghast, livid, wrenching himself free from his usual cultivated habits. He went to stand in his study for a minute, perhaps to stare at his ancestors' swords. In his own eyes he carried swords of justice. Vengeance, punishment, call it what you will. I asked if I could possibly accompany him. He snapped refusal. Sir, this was not a pleasant task; but he had to see it through to a finish. A sombre duty to be performed.

We parted. Dear God, those peasants. I had the feeling I ought to ring Robles, but that could simply widen the mischief. This was the dilemma: one shoved one's nose in, saw for an instant beneath the tourist surface, but then helpless had to take the shock. My initial reaction in Lima had been right: socially, this was a foul country.

Strange, but I felt it so deeply at that moment that my interest in Paula, who was after all herself entrenched in this order of society, snapped. Leaving her uncle's bastille in Cuzco I also cut away from her. I couldn't look her up again in Lima.

Well, such insights come and go. One records them, even if one is not consistent.

The flight across the cordillera was magnificent. Salcantay, the Savage one, was smiling. Peru was full of beauty too.

Above all, among its people.

8

THE BAPTISM

It was almost midday when I reached the house; but for once I didn't heed this, I was so excited to be back at the Señora's. "Meche!" She was sitting on a step, her legs trailing into the sunlight that was thicker and dustier than when I had left. Baby at the breast she was nonchalantly haggling with a seller of brushes, who was paying her compliments. He was standing very erect, smiling.

"Señora!" She disappeared within, to return, with little Jesús too, in the wake of their patrona. The brushman gleamed. It was a committee of reception. The Señora gripped my hand and smiled with seriousness then a gust of jollity, and she kept patting my back as we entered the house. "What a long time! What a journey you have been!" She smiled as though at times she had doubted I would return from such far-off wanderings. My room, she said, was waiting, ready. She poured me a sherry; we sat, facing. As I prattled about the beauties of the flight, the thrill of these airlifts across the mountains, the feeling of a country that had long been dormant so-to-speak picking up its bed and walking, she smiled the same steady smile of welcome. "You have so much to tell me. You are at home now." She conveyed the feeling that in part at least I had been travelling so as to relate it to her. Then firmly she said, "But first you must eat. We are only waiting for Roberto and Carmela. Then we take the comida together. Señor John." It was the big step.

From this point on I ate with them at midday.

Roberto arrived first. He was in a truculent mood. Examination time was approaching, and he viewed it with extreme distaste. Even if, with a natural facility that cancelled out half his laziness, he had learned enough to scrape through, he was loathe to offer it up to the examiners. If he knew it, he knew it. Was it their concern? He looked me over, arriving from the highlands and not yet into my city gear, as if I were some added irritation. Then as quickly it changed; he drew me to the sitting room (I had been sitting in a wicker chair on the porch) and pointed to what indeed I had noticed, a resplendent television set.

"I decided to get it." He waved towards it, negligently ignoring my attempts at praise. "Last night we watched a Bob Hope film. It's a fine set, no?" He was now more friendly. As his mother entered he embraced her. "Mother says it will ruin our credit. But she loves it so much she even no longer has time to go and see Juanita!"

"I have, Roberto! With all the preparations!"

"Mamma, I am teasing!" he corrected. He grinned. His self-esteem was now back to normal. He went up to wash, whistling a tune.

He was still up there when Carmela ran in. She flicked across the room, flicked the set on. "How can you bear to sit there and not watch it!" It was as if I had failed to pay her a compliment. A tap of heel, a dainty shrug, and she would actually have got cross with me; but, taking a leaf from their criollo habits, the digs they always got in at each other, I said that Roberto had given me the impression that only he was allowed to touch it.

"Nonsense! That is just Roberto. It's my set, you know; I insisted. Look, now we can watch some music." She threw up her elbows, took a small step, the beginnings of a paso doble, then swung at her normal pace towards me. "Aren't you glad to be back in Lima?" I said I was delighted. "I knew you would be. I told you! And think what you have missed! You sent a postcard to Macú, no?"

"As you seem to have heard . . ."

She sparkled with pleasure. Ah, la la! She was tripping from the room. "I am glad you are back, Señor John. We'll arrange"

. . . she paused, turned, for a second ceased the otherwise ceaseless flicks of movement . . . "why don't you buy a car?"

I grinned, speechless.

"That's right, you buy a car!" Like castanets, she clicked up the stairs, brisk, determined, full of fire, then outside the bathroom she shouted at Roberto.

This exuberance continued all through the meal. It was certainly the unstudied time of day, with the natural bubbling up of family affairs. To a newcomer most of it would have been meaningless, for hint followed hint in swerving succession; and even after two months with this family, a month on the spot and a month in the hinderland from which they had originated, the latter actually helping better with the deciphering of idea and response, much of it went past me. Logically, I had been excluded till now. But now all three, so individually different, drew together to make sure I felt accepted. It had been decided, so no half measures: no more than a passing nod to punctilio before "Señor" was dropped before my Christian name. They seemed to feel that having met their clan, and possessing indeed a clearer picture than they of how it all now looked in the south, having seen the ingredients that composed their soul—though the soul itself would be for ever elusive—it followed that I should be drawn in here. They sought my opinion to some extent, my backing for this declaration or that; they expected me to be equally forthcoming. This meant, also, quips, knocks, continual sly digs below the belt. I began deploying my own mild barbs.

The Señora, I hadn't realised it so strongly, adored these two young people. She was critical and fearful on their behalf, and as they skirmished with each other she did some tut-tutting; but beyond adding her recurrent plea that Carmela get home earlier of an evening—as she put it now, "you must consider how your brother feels, Carmela!"—she was benign first with one then the other. She even smiled at their jokes about Juanita, not all of which were kind. Knowing her sympathy for her elder daughter and the way her principles made her suspicious of anything reactionary, or trivial, it was surprising to see her laughing with the younger one: something that never happened at breakfast. The midday comida opened up another vein of her personality.

The food was simple; we ate hungrily. Talk never stopped. Roberto was being difficult again, or it was a mood he deployed to vex his sister. "If you weren't so mean," he sniffed at her, "we could buy the Benny Goodman record. Surely, you don't have to pay at the cinema?"

"No, but I have to wear some clothes."

"Oh?" He managed to look insulting. "Not as at these beatnik parties. Have you heard, Mamma, of the Suarez scandal? They fortunately didn't name the girls. An English pilot, John, was involved. So where did you go, Carmela, last night?"

"I?" She went scarlet. Fly though she was, she was easily disconcerted by him, "As you know. I saw the Catinflas film. Oh, I go for Catinflas. He laughs at everyone. Do you know, Señor— John, do you know . . ."

"Describe it!" He was not to be put off. "Else Mamma will think you were at one of those parties. Describe it, or I shall ring up Santiago. What will you do one day if there's a murder, and your only alibi is Catinflas? At least make it Elvis Presley! I'm beginning to doubt you still go with Santiago. We never see him. Why doesn't he propose?"

She shrugged. "He doesn't like me to work. He feels he must earn enough for two."

"So he should." The Señora nodded sagely. "And you, Roberto, where were you last night?"

"With you, here, Mamma, watching television." His most awful qualities smiled from his face.

"Yes, but that was only for an hour. And then I went over to Juanita's."

"Juanita! Juanita! Prmm-prmm, Conchita!" Conchita was to be the name of the newborn.

"At least she is giving me the grandchildren."

Roberto shrugged as though to say he could do that without noticing it, twice a night.

Carmela remarked, "They look blacker each time."

The Señora grinned. "You must redress the balance." She sucked her teeth enjoying the earthiness. She pushed the cheese in my direction. "In our family there is every colour." She sighed. "Yes. It is as it should be. Are you out again tonight, Carmela?"

Camela was wary. She glanced at Roberto. Basically, however much they tiffed, they depended utterly upon each other. He replied for her, "I am meeting Carmela in town. I shall see her safely into a cinema! Isn't Macú going with you this time?" He leered, sideways. I might have guessed that Carmela would tell him everything.

It was my turn to try a riposte.

But Roberto made circles round all of us.

Two days later he produced a car, borrowed from a man who hoped to touch him for an introduction to a certain woman. Inevitably, he was lush with the details, thoughtfully looking about my room, at my camera, at the watch on the table, to see if there was scope for further arrangements. He concluded there wasn't, put his arm on my shoulder, said that as now we were such close confidants I had only to ask . . . I understood, yes? In the meantime the car, shining at the door, was there to take us all to the beach—alas, not Carmela, poor child, her dreary bank; nor Fernando sitting for the first of his exams; but just his mother, Juanita, and I. Yes, Juanita; he had nothing against her. She was going to dump her two brats with Meche.

To his mother he had told a quite different story, but it came to the same point, he was at the wheel. He was a born driver, a mechanised horseman who charged his steed into the thick of the battle turning, at that precise moment, to pay his sister an airy compliment. Towards Juanita he was terribly correct, terribly suave, her swordsman brother. I can't say that she did more than grimace, though perhaps she did fall for it a bit; it didn't much help to know about Roberto. These women all lay down for their menfolk in the hope that they might be used as doormats. The men enjoyed the situation, though took care to be stylish about it.

On the beach, the first few groups assembling, the first toddlers, the athletes, in advance of the summer city hordes, we squatted on the wispy sand well back from the fall of breakers and watched Roberto show his paces. He walked to the sea, still the caballero, stood regarding it mournfully: was overtaken by energy, so that he moved, trotted, joined in a ball game to do some very fancy head shots. Next moment he had tired and stripping to his pants dashed headlong into the water: but thought better of it, and retreating with composure, a stroll that took him to a trio of girls above whom he placed his well-made figure, he subsided momentarily from our view. Half an hour later he was lying by himself, just beyond earshot of what we were saying. He doubtless knew we were discussing his future, doubtless expected us to be doing that; but, and it was this that tired his mother, he was so cock-certain that all would go well for him whether he, or she, did anything or not, that all he ever did was to smile indulgently and say "Mamma, there's plenty of time." He had even teased, "Let's wait for the Election!" and "Isn't it enough to be a Montellano?" That last had made her hopping mad.

All the same, feeling the warm sand beneath us and the slight summery breeze off the sea, she was relaxed to explore all these points. We were now retracing my journey to the south, for the benefit of Juanita also. There was no detail they allowed me to skip; they needed to be absorbed into those environments. They were practically interested, it struck me, with regard to the patrón, Silvestre Echarri, and the growing forces he represented; they granted him some of the love and respect still flooding about the doctor's memory; and it gratified them to hear that he was still climbing. Juanita said, though she suspected him politically, that he ought be be made a Deputy for Puno: to put a further seal on family achievement. She was glad they had chosen him as compadre for the baptism.

Yet, this said, it was just as evident that the real pull was to Arequipa. To the old couple who hadn't given recognition, who as they neared the grave in that fading city probably felt stuck in their ungracious predicament. The Señora loved and pitied her parents, and sighed openly at the waste of it all, but she said, "I understand them perfectly."

Juanita was less patient. "We should go there, Mother." After her delivery she was more forceful, ardent, full of rippling smiles, but less serene. One could see her now as the oldest child, the leader, on whom her mother rested.

"If Augusto's coming here?"

"Oh, he's an idiot."

They amiably drifted on to other topics.

"Well, who in the end will do more for Roberto—Echarri, or Augusto?"

"But Mother, I thought you had decided that! This garage Silvestre has written about. You can see Roberto understands machines."

"I wonder." The Señora retreated, refusing discussion, into some private summery dream, a dream by its depth that came from childhood.

Roberto returned. We piled into the car. They had also the keys for a house in Miraflores that Jaunita wished to see over. A removal had been decided upon, Emilio's family offering the deposit; and now it was Roberto's chance to tease her, too good to miss—"I say, Miraflores!"

"Well?"

"You will have to change your politics."

Drily, "Oh hardly, Roberto caro. Perhaps, for San Isidro or Monterrico, but as everybody knows Miraflores has gone down." She said this with such a social air that Roberto was delighted. He blew her a kiss. "I can see, you are already transformed."

Indeed, Juanita every minute looked different: or was it just seeing her away from that overcrowded stuffy flat and the hungry students and the swollen pregnancy? Brother and sister, supposedly unalike, obviously hit it off with ease.

He had to pay for this however. Carmela, returning later in the evening with some friends to watch television, learned of the excursion and was very put out. "So you become a garage hand?" she scoffed him. "You allow the chola to pull us down?" Extreme deduction though this sounded, it followed; criollos didn't waste their breath. But Roberto, equally with his second sister, had a way to put over confidence. It was a different way, less sunny; but it told her that her vulgar little fears were groundless. Roberto and Carmela stood closer to each other.

Then, poor Carmela, she had to stomach the presence of the patrón, Silvestre Echarri, and his son Julio, in the house for some days.

The baptism was approaching. Other affairs went on as usual but knitting them all was a growing excitement directed towards the coming weekend. The festivities, to be at the Señora's, had to be prepared for; and an aunt of Emilio's, chosen as godmother, the same who had fed us that Sunday in Huancayo before our disastrous night on the bus, was already installed in her niece's flat, helping with the baby and appearing each day to discuss the catering with the Señora. Compa Pau himself, inevitably with Pa Mígue, would be down Friday, so as to be drinking from the night before. It was even now rumoured Augusto was coming, a last minute concession from Arequipa; he would be staying with Paula's mother. She too would be at the church, but not at the following celebration.

It was all so exciting, even by Wednesday one could feel the extra tremor in the house; one got up to a slightly quickened day; and Meche, whose child Conceptión was to be dealt with at the same ceremony, unobtrusively for the sake of the thing, was mixing her singing with snatches of talk, pleas, prayers seemingly to the unseen spirits whom she had suddenly bethought herself might do the babes harm before the guarantees of the Catholic service. An unknown sight, she was crossing herself, and she had asked the Señora to speak to Serafino. For some days at least there was an uplifted tone.

On the Thursday evening I accompanied the Señora to her daughter's flat, as in past times: and here at first glance nothing had changed. This was amazing, for even with us Roberto and Carmela, and the studious Fernando, interspersed their concerns with thought of the party, and had begun moving the furniture to make room for the dance, brother and sister trying a few steps; but here, Conchita asleep with Manuel, and the Aunt out with other relatives, the visible scene was as before, the students talking and Emilio presiding and mother and daughter preparing soup. Emilio, of course with a new soft glow and such a quietness of authority now he had only to raise his finger for attention, smiled apologetically as if aware of some discrepancy; but said, "At least, here, we are happy; but up on the sierra how many are liable to be killed at any minute?"

They were discussing the Cerro de Pasco affair. The papers were now reporting it daily. Two hundred and fifty armed police, Guardias de Asalto, had been sent from Lima; the comuneros, the members of the Yanahuanca and Yaruscarán Communidades, who had done the invading of the land in dispute, equally had deployed themselves, under cover of night and with the use of horse, in strategically sound positions. Press photos showed the two forces, eight hundred metres apart on that scratchy land at twelve thousand feet, helmet and rifles, smoke bombs and swords at the ready on the one side, slings and clubs, wily looks and bitterness apparent from the other. The ranchers were evacuating their wives and children, and calling on the Government to stop vacillating and send the police into action; they rejected all the peasant claims, reaffirmed their titles, and looked to the law. The peasants, who no longer had faith in the law, were willing to be slaughtered rather than move. So far the Government was simply talking.

"But it can't continue talking for ever. Poor Government, for once I pity it. With elections coming it can't order a massacre, or at least its APRA contingent can't, on a scale to satisfy its instincts. Likely enough, it will pull the police back." This was a student I didn't know, a shock-haired sweatered figure who smoked and seemed not to listen to the others.

"But that is being too hopeful, Lucho. They can't accept the comuneros' case. First some leaders and a poor fish of a lawyer sent let's say to parley with officials will be thrown into prison.

Then a group of Deputies will visit. Then after weeks of manoeuv-
ring to ring every drop of political advantage for this gentleman,
or for that gentleman, reinforcements will be despatched and
. . . blood will flow."

"Yes," pronounced Emilio with almost trance-like calm, glowing yet at this point deadly, "blood will flow. Once again it will
flow, as if the police and their rifles can settle anything. Provocation from both sides, because now nothing but death satisfies.
That is the way it goes in our country." He held them silent
with the fixity of his look. "But need it? Can't we . . . intervene?
Isn't this an issue for a general strike? Through meetings . . .
couldn't we rouse . . . force—?"

"No, Emilio, hombre, no." His wife spoke with equal quietness and intensity from the background. "The law is a poor wall,
I know, against centuries of shame and neglect, but it is the law,
and you cannot support violations of it. Reform, not violence;
you yourself have always . . ." Her liquid face, gentle, pleading,
was as firm as his: continuing, it seemed, some earlier private
debate. Juanita, freed, was re-entering politics, with an eye very
likely to curbing his rashness; for Emilio looked, since I had last
seen him on the plains to the south of Ayacucho, to have moved
that much more to the left.

"So blood will flow," mused the sweatered student, addressing
some point above them on the wall, "ritual murder, burning and
beating. Let us put it in mid-March, for madness. The peasants
will be allowed to bury their dead; the landowners will rewire
their frontiers. And then what? The peasants will return. Those
comuneros will again go back. And back and back until the law
is changed. What we should do is . . . join them at it!"

I related my small experience from Cuzco, naturally without
mentioning names. Oh Cuzco, yes, they had heard of its horrors,
and of comparable horrors to the south in Puno; but what held
them this evening was the crisis in Pasco, a revolt that was sufficiently big and well-organised to have commanded the entire
nation's attention. It was not being driven back out-of-hand, as
had always happened previously. Although by March it would

certainly have been crushed, as Lucho said it would be re-created. This Pasco affair was a turning point.

"You see," said Emilio, "if only there was a leader of Tupac Amaru's stature today, then in Pasco ... Cuzco ... Puno ... the highlands as one man would rise! And the workers on the coast plantations; and the people in the barriadas! Doesn't he exist! Isn't he here, in this city? Some serrano living in this city?"

Juanita quickly brought on the soup.

Saturday, the day of the baptism, came. It started with a barrage from the radio. Roberto, a bit at a loss for once, got up too early, switched on the set, increased the volume till it began to blare like the invitation to a fairground. He switched off abruptly. He and the patrón stood exchanging cigarettes on the porch. He had been very polite, but very aloof, since yesterday to his Uncle Silvestre; it was he who acted like the man of means, the man who had some favour to dispense, but which he was not going to dispense too easily; while here in the city the powerful patrón, the coarse dark bull from the upland pastures, was careful to watch his p's and q's. This was uncertain territory for him. That was why he wanted Roberto. Roberto was to become the tutor of his son, the two of them to be partners in a garage, that he the patrón would of course control. Establish that first; much else to follow. But Roberto, leisurely, seemed not to understand.

Behind him, icily, flitted Carmela. She had stayed at home the previous evening to help her mother and the compadre from Huancayo—my extraordinary relation, she seemed to say; though towards that cheery copper-faced lady even Carmela responded with affection. But not to the patrón. He seemed to like her; he was like a visiting sheikh in the metropolis willing to add her, with others selected, to the chambers of his provincial harem. However she tried, she couldn't offend him. But for Carmela this was countryman's strategy, her uncle remained her most deadly enemy (and Carmela was one to collect quite a few): the object at stake being not just Roberto but her own most personal sense of identity. Roberto for her was a line of defence.

In asides from this imbroglio I chatted with Echarri, and was gratified to find he treated me as one who came from the hills as he did. He brought me greetings from Señor Justo. Also, as I had fulfilled his commissions, bearing gifts from Puno to Lima, he gave me now some magnificent coins, minted he said from a Montellano mine in the early days of the Republic. This was a wry thing to do, and I began to see, in his rustic way, behind those beetling fleshly features, he got quite a kick from the family situation. In fact, throughout the proceedings that followed, despite the presence in the church of Augusto and from Lima Mathilde Montellano, Silvestre Echarri, the patrón, the cholo, continued quietly to dominate. Esteban perhaps would have overshadowed him, but I never saw the two of them together.

The ceremony itself was soon over. The godmother held the baby at the font (and the Señora held Meche's babe), the priest spoke and sprinkled water and sermonised on the duties of godparents. Echarri settled the first of these, and went off to collect the certificates. Everyone marvelled. Coins were thrown to small children outside the church. A special medallion of the Virgin of Guadeloupe, for Juanita's daughter had been named Conchita Maria Guadeloupe, was given to each guest present. People loitered: Augusto and Compa Pau chatting in sheer amazement at each other. Señora Montellano stood aside with the patrón, then she and Augusto talked to our Señora, in a happy everyday manner as if for them years were no more than minutes, then those two had to go on their way. The rest of us returned to the house, where all through the day more people appeared, bringing gifts and praising what they saw, then in the evening some of them again to join in the dance.

That austere old house rocketed with noise, like a dray horse pulled into a rodeo. Whang! And the balloon went up. There were two guitarists and a small drum player, and a friend of the band with castanets, a concentrated foursome that drove their music like a drill through the neighbourhood's quiet. There was no exclusiveness to the party at this stage; if a neighbour looked in, he came in too. There was food in abundance, plates of cebiche and tamales and potato concoctions, and later anticuchos, and

then a great stew that had hotly flavoured chicken and mutton
in it; there was drink in abundance, to lift people off their feet
and get them clapping to the marinera; Huancayo and Puno
had combined to pay for all, and for more if there were more to
come who wanted it. It was the night of the open purse, without
a thought for anything but a record celebration.

Not strictly true; there are always undercurrents. I imagine the
patrón, who was leaving in the morning, wanted an answer before
he became too intoxicated. At an early stage then, after half a
dozen glasses, just nicely warming up on the outskirts of a polka
he placed his proposition before the Señora. (We were to hear the
details recited by her again and again in the following days.) He
had improved his offer: as well as the garage they would buy a
fleet of collectivos. His cousin Justo would be there to help.
Roberto would work in each section in turn, then direct it and
then, but here time was left vague, become half owner of the
joint business. It was extraordinary the faith he had in Roberto;
it was this perhaps that unsettled the Señora, made her doubt his
ultimate intentions, In any case it was a far cry from building
roads or bridges or dams, the dream her husband had had for
their son, to messing about with cars in Lima. It was still something
"cholo", but without the vision. Emphatically, she was not
interested.

Roberto was suddenly. Did he smell the money, the youthful
power and the easy life? Never mind the oft-repeated prejudices
or what Carmela was going to say, he wanted to be in that
garage. He could see now, he was made for cars! This was what
he said, flushed, when he was asked by his mother, formerly, for
his views.

But was Roberto in fact still gambling, with an inborn and
unscrupulous astuteness? Had he seen that she was against it, and
against it now for some other reason, hardly as yet apparent to
herself but to do with yearning again for Arequipa and with meeting Mathilde and Augusto and feeling that finally that was where
she belonged? I am anticipating slightly, for these feelings of hers
became visible to all on succeeding days but were not clear on the

day of the baptism. It was to become visible that Carmen Maria Echarri, the Montellano girl who three decades before had broken out of her family for love, for love mixed with fighting principles, had aged and quietened (and perhaps felt lonely) and, although still proud of her own action, no longer wanted her son Roberto, the youngest and weakest chick of her brood, to move further into the cholo orbit. It was enough that he was mestizo to his fingertips; for the rest let him be a Montellano, be schooled and found occupation by them. This was a volte-face for the Señora, but so convinced did she become of it it must have been maturing for some time within her life.

Emilio was to say, commenting on it, that it had begun that night she had gone to the police, and then, desperate, cap in hand to Carlos.

But, as I say, on the day of the baptism no one, except possibly Roberto with his feline intuition, had much clue to this change within her; it was taken for granted, and by Carmela with harshness, that the Señora must accede to Echarri, for he was the head of the clan and also offering to house them more comfortably in Lima. Bandit though he might be up on the sierra, he was behaving like a prince in the city. This was the current direction of his bounty. And as the dance proceeded, swirling and stamping to the talkative rhythm of the criollo waltz, he stood there acclaimed in the background as the Good Father Christmas of them all.

The Señora said no. She had decided, no. She explained that it was to do with her husband's last wishes. Roberto was to become an engineer, and if he failed, as was likely, his exams in Lima, then he must go to the States to study there.

Roberto took the cue. He could evaluate "States". It meant Carlos in the picture, more money still, and a Montellano future. Interest in the garage evaporated; he was next seen dancing with one of his muchachas, a real "planera" as he blandly termed her; half an hour later he had gone for the night. He did not return before the patrón's departure.

Echarri took this setback well. At first he pretended not to believe it, and polished off more food and drink. He was conviviality itself to everyone. He laughed at the idea that Roberto could refuse him. But all the same, he took his measures, and next drew Emilio aside. Emilio had cousins with a finger in transport and like anyone else could be a businessman when it came to the interests of his family. Something was discussed, but about then too the patrón succumbed to the alarming quantity of neat spirit he had been tossing back, so perhaps the discussion did not go far. It was never in any case referred to again. In the following days when the Señora was talking she never mentioned this other possibility. She was not interested apart from Roberto.

Juanita had others things to talk about, and soon Emilio had too.

Carmela rejoiced; then forgot all about it, for . . . Santiago's boss had raised his salary! So now she agreed: he had to propose to her! All night at the dance she had clung to her lover, applying herself with hectic gaiety. Her every movement had craved for attention. Juanita, who was perfectly good-natured, had not suppressed a dry smile. "You'll wear yourself out, Carmela dear!" "Oh, but don't you like my dress? Aren't you happy tonight?" Carmela, in her transports, had a naïve sweet voice; she had clicked away and, re-entered the dance.

Macú asked, "Can you do the marinera? You must watch. I shall dance it now with my brother." The rhythm had sped into a fast run, with a finger-snapping staccato drum beat and high teasing guitar notes into which a singer's voice fitted, calling out it was the marinera! He was continuing some ditty about it, a high flamenco chatter of words, then he broke off to a drumming handclap and acclaimed! Macú and her brother had taken the floor.

They saluted, and moved apart, always to this teasing tripping rhythm, circling at opposite ends of the room, then back they came towards each other weaving a cautious cunning course in preparation for the main encounter.

"Mándame quitar las vida . . . si es delito el adorarte . . . que yo no seré el primero . . . que muera por ser tu amante . . ." The singer spoke the man's desires.

Macú in a dress that twirled around her, her left hand plucking its hem, was very coquettish, full of mischief; and he was tall, like a matador, slim, turning in the smallest circle, but guileful and varying his approach with something of negro nonchalance. The dance came from the Spanish zamacueca and had little passes from the bullring in it, but also much of local adornment, of mestizo mimicry and humour. Most delightful of all was the play of handkerchiefs, held by each in the right hand, held aloft or whisked sideways or sailing nimbly out of reach. At moments they flagged the air with messages, then repeated the limpid statuesque circling as another close engagement was broken off. The man displayed his best paces, acclaimed her beauty, ployed her with compliments; she in turn half-surrendered, retreated, then gave and took something from the moment of shared victory. Acclaimed, he the victor and yet the vanquished, they finished in a fury of heel stamps and small fluttering toe movements. They sailed away; the singer ended his expostulatory staccato story, and as the dance concluded and we all applauded, the guitars were plucked meditatively for a moment then were strung again to the high commencement, and the drum tapped out the rhythm. Two other dancers took the floor.

Some of the guests began to leave. It could not be an all-night party. Juanita collected her baby and Manuel from somewhere at the back where Meche was attending to them and, sleepy-eyed, they were taken home. For an hour or more still the marinera continued, then the waltz, mambos, a dreamy blues, in which the usual joker switched out the lights, tangos: all of which fitted the occasion, but none so well as the marinera. In that was expressed the douceur de vivre that this city, for all its anxieties, passed on to each generation.

Sleep well, little Conchita.

Mischievous, radiant-hearted Macú.

The party, the little "jarana", was over. The women were clearing. The last guest had eaten his fill and departed. In the room the Señora moved to and fro, full of newborn resolution.

9

A MOMENT OF CRISIS

THE following week I had lunch with Carlos. His letter suggested I should meet him at his office. When I showed it to the Señora and asked her about him she said she liked him best of the Montellanos; in a general sense he was the most intelligent, not so committed as people supposed, free still within himself and brave enough to put conscience or concept of public service before his own or the family's interests. This was unusual in his milieu. It might come from his English education, the cricket field and his tutor at Oxford; and in part as reaction from his father's methods, that embraced everyone in a bearlike hug at the same time parting them from half their wealth. At thirty-five he was the eldest child of Mathilde and Esteban. Paula came next; well, I knew her. Then there was Victor, an army officer, very serious and not at all political. Then Pedro, a would-be diplomat, who saw his career as the pursuit of women. Then Consuelo Rose. Of these, Carlos clearly was the foremost.

His office was a tower of glass. The family owned the entire building. He was near the top, the captain on the bridge, for already it was he, more than Esteban, who piloted their daily affairs. Esteban, so the Señora had told me, had had a run of crazes the last few years that had taken him all over the world; while Carlos strongly at this moment felt one had to stick to Peru. Sink or swim—though in fact the Montellanos had property and cash in both the States and Europe. They would always swim; but at least Carlos felt that one had to devote every ounce of one's energy to making sure the country swam also. At the last, if it ever came to that point, he might elect to stay and sink; he was unpredictable—well, they all were that; it was a Montellano trait. (The Señora, with her own new decisions, had pronounced this a trifle smugly.) And then, as he didn't get on with his wife and disliked being seen about with her, the office provided a refuge. He was happiest there. Ring him at any hour of the day, and on any topic, he would gladly add it to his overloaded schedule.

I got out of the lift a floor too soon and padded up the humming staircase. Picture of walls, brick doorways, and secretaries with lingering curves. Animation in glass cubicles. Suggestion of it being I can't think what. Then a very homely woman receiving me and ushering me into the master suite, where one could stand sit, or lie full length with equal comfort and appropriateness, and digest the paintings or a volume of Shakespeare and of course, the sherry she had already poured, but from where the impulse was mainly outward: out across the sky and this sprawling city, to understand it or to pulverise it. Height of this sort had to be used.

I had time to reflect that Carlos hadn't built it. He might use it as simply as others a bus. It must be he who had introduced the Shakespeare, alongside the numbers of *Fortune*.

He had the Montellano features, broad, broken up, without the pugnacity of his father. He came in smiling, he had a friendly personality, but he was not in the least a jolly man. He wore spectacles, he was heavily built, he had a look that was keen and energetic, and detachedly amused at moments in a way that recalled Paula, but most of all he looked tired, pressed, yet able to see it through. He could have been an English civil servant. Speaking, the slight drawl in his voice, the years of precise negotiation, he became more English still. He didn't seem a Latin American, except for his colouring, even there toned down, and certain movements of his arms that suggested moments of chaotic upheaval.

He joined me in a sherry. "It was very nice of you to come. Paula seemed to think I might be of some use to you. Your 'researches'? Are you spying out the land?"

I gave some feeble explanation, noting this latest manoeuvre of Paula's. By now I knew exactly what my intention was with regard to Peru (I had known it from the moment Azuarga had nudged me), but as yet I hadn't the nerve to declare it.

"I see. You might write a book about us?" He went past evasion straight to the core. "You would have to make that pretty strong . . . take your courage in your hands. Please, come here." He drew me to the window, to the dizzy frontage overlooking the city. I think, in a flash, whatever the problems he had been dealing with two minutes before, he was already into the feel of my project, trying it for himself, interested.

We could see into other ordinary offices, and into the glass boxes of competing skyscrapers. Lima was climbing to the skies apace. He selected one, where we could see a gentleman also staring out of his window.

"That gentleman there, Señor X. . . . I don't think you ought to omit him! I know him; for all he's a business man, he has an antiquated psychology. He clings to the advantages of Spanish laws designed for an earlier century, that allow him to abuse the investing public. He lobbies for high tariff protection, that allows him to sell mediocre products. Too expensively. He and his friends anonymously share an interest in several firms, none today of an economic size, nor on good terms with their labour force. The management is poor because he lives in Lima, while the factories themselves are all near Ica; and his main concern, apart from profit, is to collect the money deferred from wages, about fifty per cent for indemnities and so on, to double its value in land development. Taxes? It is easier to bribe. So finally he manages, and I happen to know there are fifteen hundred such gentlemen in Lima, to pocket ten thousand pounds per year. It could be more.

"So, spare a thought for him. Above all, for his psychology." Carlos smiled wistfully, beginning, I think, to entertain himself.

He drew me back towards a settee. Sitting close, nodding sagely, a laconic glimmer underlining that it was a performance, just one approach among many to the subject that in my shoes he was now trying out, he continued, "As with master, with man. Labour is as rigid. The aim is security—not qualifications, or improvement through a free contract position. Productivity is low, though I maintain our workers could be as industrious as any. They are immobilised by fear, by the thought of the pension and other benefits that eventually accrue most likely by sitting as quietly as possible. They are not protagonists of change. Least of all could you convince a white collar man that he and the country would be healthier if he was a mechanic or an electrician, and incidentally earned twice as much. I needn't underline that.

"But, spare a thought for him . . . and see how Peru perspires even as it tries to breathe. Like someone who clings to winter clothes on a warm summer's day."

He paused, then "I won't include the Government . . . for the Government being the main subject of the Press you must have noted the mentality for yourself. It stifles every department. It has become a function of government as such . . .

"Though . . . not all is black there. In finance, a beginning. A basis on which advance can be made. One merely shudders at what waits to be done and the paucity of time in which to do it. That's why I stress psychology." He paused, then added—"And in the realm of government, this now has become paramount. For it is the Government, co-opting capital and labour, taxing those private export empires, reasoning with foreign capital also, that has to revolutionise Peru. We have very largely to act as Communists, but of course not become that!"

He smirked, broke off. "You must forgive me lecturing. I haven't yet really come to the point. If you're going to do a book, though, you must occasionally be grim. And the grimmest thing here is . . . the land question. The man who owns it, and the man who does not—the locked conflict between the two of them: the ultimate static situation. There lies the root of our psychology. That is why we are as we are, you know. Bust that, and advance is possible. Nothing less will work."

I asked him, "Do you proclaim this openly? I would expect it more from the extreme left—"

"From your friend Emilio?" Something less friendly came into his eyes.

"Why, yes?" I was suddenly worried. For behind the reasonable tones of Carlos and this attitude he was trying out were all the visible signs of power, the power to fix the rules of the game. His look, however, cloaked over at once. He said, "The most usual attitude, in Lima, is 'Apres moi, le déluge'! But some of us think, accepting the deluge, that it is better we who bring it about! Land has to be radically re-apportioned, to start the process off. Cash must flow into everybody's hands, to create the national size market that, as you know, today is non-existent. We need every Peruvian inside the economy. Everybody needs food and education—well, you know it all: but what I am saying, the engineering of this process is vital. In the wrong hands it could go worse than wrong."

"Which party, then, do you favour as—?"

"Oh, the politicians! Let them hold the fort, do the explaining to the Americans and so on. The laws we need are largely enacted: all we require is a central committee, a National Agrarian Institute, etc., quietly told it can go ahead. Don't mistake me: the outcome would be radical. I am not suggesting evasive measures. No; but I want it done impersonally, scientifically."

"What are the chances?"

"I am optimistic."

He returned to the window. "Señor X. has gone. If we meet him at lunch I must introduce you. For, though we have other types of business men, Yankee-style exporters, plantation owners who are absolutely up to the minute—well, the best in fact are our Americans—and then of course people like my father, who help for they amass capital for the country, the average, the typical man of affairs still has Señor X.'s mentality. Even Lima on average, psychologically, is still in the thirties. Come, it's time to go to the Club."

"So you see what I mean," he said in the lift, a private lift off a different corridor, "those students in the streets, those land-invading comuneros, they simply stiffen the issues. They toughen the old psychology, of which to my mind they are equally the product. They slow down what has to be done."

"In Cuba they were successful!"

"Peru is not Cuba." He smiled grimly. "Our impatient friends have got to see that." The grimness stayed just long enough to show that Carlos, in the higher interest, wouldn't balk at strong measures.

We lunched at the elegant Club Nacional, a magnified hacienda house, off good complicated French food. At our backs the Plaza San Martin twirled with arriving and departing collectivos, and the sudden sorties of shoeshine boys, and a sleepy policeman, but few other people, for the summer heat was gathering now. Longer lunchtimes, and a seawards dash before getting back to the office. In a club like this it made for more deliberation, another sherry, and a second helping; groups of men, their expressions humming with political expectation, lit extra cigars. From the outer world came a muffled explosion and the sudden raised clamour of sirens—a riot, possibly? A building collapsed? It could have been the revolution itself. In here one didn't worry, the immediate concern was to choose one's lunch well.

Carlos talked about his years in England, and travels round the European continent, revealing a young idealistic self that momentarily crept into his features. Those had been the wonderful idle years, although in fact he had slogged pretty hard; in fact he couldn't remember a time when it had not been bed and work for him! Hardly the Latin American image; but then he had been born to wealth, responsibility, it meant even while playing one played hard; it was the poor—well of course they slaved at it, too . . . but one could see the appalling difference, couldn't one? Though, the more he thought about the peasants, Indians, colonos or "yanaconas" as they called them, say sixty per cent of Peru's population with an average annual income of fifteen pounds, millions of semi-drugged faces slaving hopelessly up there on the sierra, the more permanently he felt bound up with them. Working like a madman in his glass tower, using the Montellano wealth where he could for long-term social investment, his eye was fixed on the lowly Indian, fellow citizens as they had to be. Make no mistake, when he spoke of reform, he meant what others called a revolution.

But no Communists . . . students . . . all those amateurs; they had to keep out of it.

He looked round. No Señor X. yet.

"Well give me your impressions," he said. He guided me, he didn't want my theories; he wanted me to talk about people, and situations met in his country. He lapped up descriptions of Augusto and Echarri. He nodded agreement about the feel of Cuzco. "You know," he said, "there's your book, isn't it? You write about the Montellanos. About us and those cholos we've collected from Puno. I'm serious. Don't laugh. Do you think we'd be offended? I can see my mother, for instance, ordering fifty copies!"

He looked impatient, the sudden turbulence within him. Was I still hesitating? It was only a detail. Only bores deliberated details. Time already to have moved on to three more.

So we moved on. Settled.

(Though afterwards alone again, and for weeks in a writer's chin-stroking haze, I envied him, and all men of affairs, that speed of decision so nicely backed up by staff to see to the execution.)

"One factor," he said, as we reached the coffee, "that we, you, must not overlook when touching upon reform in Peru, is that we are not the first to begin. I mean, Mexico, Bolivia, Cuba, and perhaps the most serviceable of all, Venezuela, have already tackled the land question. Mexico, the oldest, since 1917, has shown, despite a rather outworn belief in the continuing value of Comunidades or 'ejidos' as they are called there, that to re-allot land acts as a catalyst. More stable and representative government follows, more cash flows, there is an industrial upsurge. A cultural renaissance, in the case of Mexico. In Bolivia, although economically chaotic, because it lacked initial planning, the Indian farmer has come into his own, and La Paz is certainly more lively intellectually. Schools and teachers alone have doubled. But Bolivia, and Cuba, are not my models—though in Cuba I like the degree of power given to the central Institute: for me Venezuela is the most interesting. There it is proceeding calmly, logically—backed up I grant by oil revenues, but also by expert initial planning. You must look into that. You'll see what I mean. Japan too is an interesting model. We do not lack examples to go by, to shape our own decisive steps. I don't, however, think much of the plan the Conservatives here produced last year, though it did run to two hundred and ninety-four articles. I am speaking of serious measures."

Cigars, a liqueur. He settled the bill. He had to chase back to the office. "You can ring me for anything, at any time. Is there, perhaps, at this particular moment . . . ?"

It was required of me to mention something. I said I had not yet travelled up the coast, to the states within a State, as I'd heard them described, of the large sugar plantations.

"But you must!" He looked round the Club, spotted a gentleman, to whom at once he took me over. He said in an aside, "Could you leave for there tomorrow?" It was as much an order as his first remark.

He introduced me to a splendid person, scion of a family that had produced Presidents, and they settled the matter in a few friendly words, for this gentleman owned a large sugar estate. I would be met, shown round, given hospitality; they had both been at Oxford, but now speaking together they larded their speech with a local touch of exquisiteness, as if the object in question was not just an Englishman, and therefore without question okay, but secretly no less than the Shah of Persia.

Carlos added, as we made for the door, "While you are up there you'd better do other estates. I'll fix it. Give me a ring at five." He mentioned the estate where Fernando came from; and when I said so—"Oh you mean that trouble-making student?" I said on the contrary Fernando was the type of young Peruvian he would most approve of. He took it in. "He must come and see me then. And by the way, between ourselves" . . . he smiled, pondered . . . "no, I mustn't spoil your book. Whatever happens, put it down." Enigmatically, he left some warning in the air.

Socialist-Tory, Establishment rebel, emotive intellectual, bound by nobody so that nobody not even himself could say where the foreseeable changes would take him, Carlos Montellano went back to his office. A millionaire's office at that.

I returned to Lima the following Sunday on the late afternoon flight. The dancing heat of the desert was fading to pink slag and trains of dust where the road traffic raced to its horizon. The mountain ribs were cloaked in mist. We flew just off the coast, sailing from one small delta to the next, a two hour spin south. The night before at the Trujillo Sports Club, on an open air floor among the trees, tricked out with coloured lights and the coloured silks and white of the dresses, and to an energetic talkative band, the marinera had been flying again. Wary smiling-hearted approach, flourish and frantic signalling of handkerchiefs, then nimbly away for the next encounter. Prologued by mambos and criollo waltzes, excuses for the maximum of body move-ment, it had come as the high spot of the evening; while all around sat mothers and aunts, and grandmothers, and small cousins. Middle class Trujillo was still one family, what Lima had been forty years before: before the hectic invasion from the provinces.

But that invasion was likely to increase. Beneath the nostalgic criollo north of plantation life and cobbled towns fluttering in the cool of evening—in any case bridge and bingo now claimed as being "the expression of our criollo soul"—there was lack of work and food and hope. From the estates and villages workers looked to Trujillo, from Trujillo to the capital. The downcoast migration was nearly as sizeable as the flow in from the sierra. And as Azuarga had brought to my attention there, a similar link of clubs in Lima existed for people from the coastal back-ground, reporting back to village or district, establishing patterns of behaviour for the next wave of immigrants. This was the outstanding social feature of present day Peru: the unofficial mass education in the habits of the capital.

Yet noting this and its logical progression to an increasingly

Yankee way of life, there was still the undeclared factor: the effect that an awakened Indian mind, with political power and based on the highlands, the coast and the jungle to either side, would have on slowing or changing the process. Though when that became a possibility, the time for it might already have gone: Robles and his vengeful Indian future might have become another might-have-been. In the meantime there were some, like Azuarga, like Emilio and Juanita, who lived with both cultures contending in their hearts and did not suppress either. They were finally despite individual quirks the easiest to talk with. One could presuppose anything, they were evenly prepared.

Though that was not to say they remained inactive in the political affairs of the day. Far from it. As soon was to show up more critically.

It was six in the evening when I reached the house. I was holding back a bit from arrival, as all downcoast I'd tried to slow the flight, for this was my last return to the Señora's. It had been my last look at Peru, scooping up the centuries as much as the distance, for from the air the Incas, or the Mochica culture, and the present time were cheek by jowl; that tiny speck down there, man, no better aclimatised. Perhaps this century would see the major changes. That or a sprawl of blood on the map.

Five more days and I should be off to England, five days that would go like minutes in the saying of Limeñan goodbyes, to land me home for Christmas Eve. So every detail now was precious. Every repetition of familiar habit, familiar not because I had been here long but because the experience had been intense.

Meche. Meche as expected was sitting on the doorstep, with babe, and Jesús playing below, and a man affably entertaining her. Governments would rise and fall, while Meche got on with the business of life, producing children and cooking food. I had once asked her if she missed her village. It was as though she had never thought of the question. She had grinned, gaining time till words would occur to her that would save having to think at all—"Mire, Señor, I have my children. My mother is dead. I have a brother who works in the Señora's cousin's garden. There are people, gente, who come to talk to me. Mucho pueblo aqui! E siempre cambiando! . . . and always changing!" She had laughed at her frankness. If the nationwide movement with its economic origin and incalculable consequences of peasants into Lima meant any-thing to Meche it meant this . . . more passing caballeros! Change brought the whole of Peru to the doorstep.

The Señora, she told me, was not at home; with Señor Roberto she had gone out visiting. This was not a repetition of habit, and a sign that this household too was moving on. Selfishly perhaps the loving observer would like what he has known to stay fixed, as the image of it will stay fixed in his mind; but already the shift in the Señora's feelings brought to the surface since the day of the baptism had been voiced enough for one to feel in touch whatever that brave person did next. I was glad I had seen that she could change course; it filled out her humanity further. Finally the image one retains of a place and of events there is not so much either of them as the human beings who give them meaning. For me Peru was firstly the Señora, the good mother housing her brood and underwriting their aspirations, while the menfolk got on with the rest of it.

I washed, changed, came down to television—one of those endless American serials exported to all corners of the globe; and next minute Fernando appeared. He had been in his room, swat-ting as usual, for the next morning's final paper; but now his inturned face was asking, how had I found his family? I had in fact brought him a gift parcel; for Fernando in the long vacation to come was staying in Lima to help with research in the university laboratories. The reports on him had been so excellent, the company was only too glad to pay; he was for them a brilliant investment.

"I agree," I told him, "with everything you said! If only Peruvian and other companies would follow the lead set by your company—on whose airline, incidentally, I fly out next Friday—the country at a bound, in that one sphere, would be a model of capitalist enterprise. But you remember Baldo, your friend, his feelings? I'm afraid I echo those, too."

We left it at that; Fernando had been reading, presumably at some early hour of morning, Spengler's *The Decline Of The West*, and it was this more than the grind of exams or controversy over the sugar empires, whether or not they ought to be nationalised or run on a syndicalist basis, that was teasing him. Had I read the book? Could I help him to formulate the questions to which it seemed to give rise, that then together perhaps we could answer? He has also been dipping into Goethe, Nietzsche . . .? Fortunately we were saved by the Señora's return.

Small, round, gently flustered, but this time it transpired from a cocktail too many, she led her son into the room. He too glowed with enchantment, and a more peremptory air than usual, like a cavalry officer of an occupying force. He swept his mother into a chair. He took over—"Just been to Mathilde's for cocktails. Everyone there. Paula asked after you." This quite extraordinary speech from him, its tone, its familiarities, the way he loosely swung away as though the best part must keep till later, reduced me to a feeble, "Mmm, how nice." I glanced at the Señora; she was smiling vacantly. Fernando was frowning into space. "Yes," said Roberto, unable to retain it, unable ever to hold anything back, "I shall be off to the States after Christmas. Mathilde's going to fix it with Carlos. He will have to see to the details." And he added a edge of contempt to his tone, as though to settle with that business man.

He smiled at the array of photographs, the assembled family who must now defer to their youngest and most gilded member, then "Hello, Fernando," and he left the room. "Excuse me, I'm already late," he cried from the hall. He swung upstairs, then he seemed to stay for ages in the bathroom.

"Goodbye," he cried, appearing again, a rather more ruthless look on his face. He swept us with a glance that took in no one. "Adios, Meche." He had gone down the street.

The Señora was asking me about the north, putting together a careful conversation. Sobering, she looked tired and grave. She had never been to that part of Peru. She knew only Lima and the south. "And now," she added, in a non sequitur, "both

my sons will be to the north. Will Roberto come back from the
States? I seem to go to so much trouble only to be left alone in the
end." She shrugged. "He was really awful at the party. Fortunately, Mathilde had given her word. Because Carlos" . . . she
stood up, steadying herself . . . "had refused."

"He wouldn't back Roberto?" Curiosity impelled me to ask.

"No. He had refused. He doesn't like Roberto . . . or, actually,
what he said to me was, 'Roberto ought to go into that garage'.
Carlos seems to hear about everything. Anyway, now . . ." She
frowned, dismissing the last vapours of the Montellano cocktails.
Her pride was making her declare this to us, but it was also
making her suffer. What price her decision? Had it simply
been weakness? She looked at us steadily, her thoughts transparent. She was suffering and yet she was still on course—finally
she had enough faith in herself. Enough Montellano resolution.

"It will be for the best," she pronounced firmly.

When Fernando had left us she asked if I was going along with
her to Juanita's. By now this had become a superfluous question. I
always went with her to Juanita's.

"No, Señora, this evening I can't. I am going to the cinema."

Surprised, very slightly as if I too had reached the point of
letting her down, she said, "Oh!" Then smiled, "I imagine you
must have telephoned from Trujillo!"

"That is clever of you. In fact, I did."

"John, it is time you were returning to England."

"It is harmless enough. You know her too. Macú has fixed
ideas on the English; she would not allow me to alter those."

The Señora slowly shook her head. Then, "My feeling is, we
are just getting to know you . . . and suddenly you want to
run away!"

"Señora, I also feel it strongly." I made a gesture of despair.
We smiled. A seal put upon our friendship.

So I didn't in those penultimate days go with her to Juanita's;
I only heard, over the comida, of the mounting tensions and
anxieties there. They arose from Emilio's tussling with his co-n
science, or tussling with some wildness that had seized him. The

Señora ranged in her evaluation. And all her reporting was interspersed with what Juanita was saying to him, and with what she herself was advising, so that one could imagine the poor man now having difficulty in distinguishing just what it was he was combating. These families discussed everything together. Individualist though each might be he had to take the hammering of the others' views, till in the end he was as much against his kin as against a particular event or policy. Of course Juanita, moderate by nature, was doubly so following the arrival of the baby. She was finding herself short of milk, and this was causing her distress, and any sudden folly on the part of her husband, who had been such a level, quietly confident man, was not to be thought possible by her. In addition it threw out of balance the structure of those student evenings: the hot-headed youngsters, the sagacious teacher. If Emilio now was as mad as they, the sessions deteriorated into a riot.

He had to regain control of himself.

"I have warned him," commented the Señora gravely, "he could end up like his father. It is one thing, and a very necessary one, to oppose injustice; it's another to plan these violent reprisals. It is not as if he were a Communist. He assures us that he is not a Communist. If he were, he says, he would return to APRA, and dissemble: that is the Party line. I don't understand Emilio at the moment."

"Mamma, those two"—for Carmela indifferently made no distinction between Juanita and Emilio—"are furious at what you have done for Roberto. Don't you see? You made a decision against them. They are furious, they—"

"No, what nonsense . . ."

But Carmela flicking her butterfly remarks and her mother's protest equally aside, having planted her one small dart, with an "Oof! these discussions!" and a searching in her handbag for a handkerchief continued quickly with an alert sweetness, "Mamma, with José and Roberto in the States, if I were to take a job there too, wouldn't you rather live there yourself? Couldn't we move there, all together?"

"I do not think I shall ever leave Lima . . . no. Only for a visit. Which I have promised José."

"Ah, caramba!" Carmela had just noticed a mark on her new white shoes. Full of little irritations she left us.

Her mother was pensive for some moments.

Roberto was not with us that day. His exams over (it was not certain that he had attended them all), he was on the beach, at Ancón, with friends. Some smart friends he was collecting.

The Señora huddled into herself. The silent house. The years ahead. The day of the baptism had been more of a milestone than she could have envisaged. She said aloud, "I had to do it. The otherway would not have suited him. In the United States he will learn to work. No, it is not that . . ." She sighed quietly. "Oh, if it's not one thing it's another!"

On the Thursday, the day before I had to leave, I paid a farewell call on Paula. I had to thank her for the gift she had made me: the gift of my experience of Peru. (I doubt it could have come about otherwise.) She laughed when I said it, brushing it aside. "Now Carlos tells me you are putting us in a book. That must mean you don't like us." Her dry, hard, gloomy manner barely concealed some personal question; but she chose between the various feelings in the air, decided on the one that was nearest to reality, a vague fading away of interest, and led upstairs where, natural hostess, she had already made sure of her cousin Enrique, the painter who at the first had brought me to her.

He was the same: black jeans, rapier manner, soft feline turn of speech. Greetings over, and some words of surprise that I had in the meantime travelled through the country, for, for him, the recent past was a continuous moment, with, he granted, some meals thrown in, in which he had been exploring the significance of a line moved slightly to the left on his canvases. Surely, he hadn't been ten weeks at that! He made me feel more than I usually did, and do now with this book nearing completion, that ten weeks is really no time at all: only time for a very tentative offering.

When I returned that evening to the Señora's, Meche told me

I must hurry over to the Brozas household. Something to do with Señor Emilio. Our Señora had left the message.

At Juanita's I found a scene of confusion and dismay. Juanita, fundamentally so balanced, was awry with tears and unrelated movements. She didn't seem to know what she was doing. Her gentle face was squashed and haggard. The Señora, so white it was alarming, was sitting very still in a chair. The compadre Vicente was trying to reassure them, and the student Lucho, the casual detached one, sat in a corner stratching his head. Both children were crying in the bedroom. Juanita went in to soothe them, came out and closed the door, went back and stayed there weeping.

The compadre said, "It is not so serious. Emilio will be back here before bedtime. Señora, may I say . . . this will pull him up a bit!" The compadre gave a short nod of common sense.

"My cousin Carlos must think that, too. I am certain, that is Carlos's opinion." She directed on us a steady look, remote, uncommunicative.

"What has happened?"

The compadre gave a shrug. "Emilio . . . well, already last Friday at the Beltran meeting he had a brush with the police. He was there with those crazy students of his. Since then, you see he is much involved with this Frente de Liberacion Nacional that is being formed from certain left-wing groups, and he has held a public meeting that was strongly subversive. The argument that our society rests on violence, a sort of frozen violence, and can therefore with honour be violently overthrown is not one that, for instance, General Cuadra appreciates. So this evening the police came here for Emilio. He refused to go with them; so they got rough. I fear" . . . he looked concernedly at the Señora . . . "it was not very nice."

There was an anguished pause. One could hear the sobs and sniffs from the bedroom.

"You think they are going to release him tonight?"

"We do not know. They only took him for questioning. He

went and made it worse for himself. But Señora Echarri has phoned her cousin."

"My cousin was completely non-committal. He did not seem —well, he was not surprised." Her voice, surprisingly, for once was hard, clipped, and louder at the finish. It was more of Mathilde Montellano's voice. The Señora was wrestling within her being.

Of course, Carlos . . .

Such opposed points of view: the millionaire planner not willing to let, perhaps particularly annoyed by this, one of his relatives set up in opposition, in quite such public fashion, anyway. A warning. But how could they stop Emilio? Prison . . . exile . . . ultimately, death: one could see how these women were already extending it. As with Emilio's father, and grandfather. What so especially would save him? They were realists.

Except, of course, himself. Emilio.

So that when miraculously into an astonished room Emilio quietly walked, with a scar and a bruise across his cheek but otherwise no worse for wear, then after the first gasps and cries and touching of him to make sure he was real the long steady looks were fixed on him: did he appear to have learned his lesson? He smiled at his mother-in-law's remonstrances, and at his wife's wet haggard gaze. "If they wish to silence me, they must put me in prison!" The compadre gave a shrug of despair. "Or send me into exile! Or, we could go by ourselves!" The Señora let out an "Ah!" of comprehension. The story would unfold as she feared. She finished it for him. "Or they could shoot you," she said.

"Yes," he agreed quietly, "they may have to do that. In the long struggle that lies ahead." I think he was enjoying the romance of it a little; though superficially he was very grave, and shocked obviously from his experience.

"What do you expect of me?" he began arguing rapidly with uanita. "Do you ask me to sit here, afraid?" Polemics flew thick and fast. Emilio was as logical as ever: only his reading of events had changed. He brushed aside pleas of wife and child. Honour was the basic emotion. Not to stick to the truth one had seen was unthinkable for a man.

He rounded on me. "I assure you, my friend, they will not give up without a fight. The parallel now is with 1809—Election or no election, it's the same. You have learned whom I mean by 'they' in Peru."

"But you used to believe in the power of morality, of inevitable progress through technology, of world opinion . . . has all that changed so abruptly, Emilio? And even if you're right, or were wrong before, isn't it wiser to prepare more cautiously, so as to be ready for a decisive moment? Like this you give the game away."

He smiled sceptically. "You too! That is exactly what Azuarga has been saying."

"Azuarga?"

"They pulled him in this evening. He pretended not to know why. He always says he is neutral in politics. Do you believe it?"

"I have my suspicions. But he's right; he lives to fight another day."

Emilio threw up his hands. He was tired. "So, if all the family is against me!" He put an arm round Juanita. "We will talk about it. I will think about it."

Over the bowl of soup that followed Emilio seemed to be feeling his way back to a more balanced appraisal of his actions, and of the realities of the political scene. The other way had not been his style fully enough for him to be convinced by it: more it had been a necessary fling, an overflow of exasperation at words and more words while up on the sierra people were being killed. (As expected there, in the last ten days, some of the Comunidades leaders had been thrown into prison; and by now, as I come to the end of this book, the police, in a force of five hundred men and headed by a Colonel, have struck and a reported number of eighteen comuneros have been shot. Much horror besides. Emilio had foreseen it.)

So how was he finally to plot his course? Of all the family he was the purest, the most led by the needs of his compatriots. He lacked Carlos's energetic power and grasp of economic possibilities, but of the two he had the finer conscience, and more heart. He suffered with others. As with his students, so Juanita and the Señora turned to him finally for the word to go by. What had he to say, once supper was over?

Nothing dramatic, only this, with a profound gentleness towards his wife, "We will talk about it together, Juanita. We can't run from trouble if it's there on our path . . . but together, I promise . . . a little more patiently. We'll find together . . ." And he included the Señora in a quiet amen of gaze and gesture.

He had accepted: three heads were wiser than one. Decisions rested within the family.

The Señora sighed with some thankfulness. At least, a truce, a chance of continuity.